I WAS THERE

GIGS THAT CHANGED THE WORLD

I WAS THERE

GIGS THAT CHANGED THE WORLD

MARK PAYTRESS

CASSELL
ILLUSTRATED

I was there

GIGS THAT CHANGED THE WORLD

First published in Great Britain in 2005 by Cassell Illustrated,
a division of Octopus Publishing Group Limited,
2–4 Heron Quays, London E14 4JP

Text copyright © 2005 Mark Paytress
Design and layout copyright © 2005 Cassell Illustrated

Distributed in the United States of America by
Sterling Publishing Co., Inc., 387 Park Avenue South,
New York, NY 10016-8810

A CIP catalogue record for this book is available from the British Library.

Editor: Joanne Wilson
Picture Research: Zoe Holtermann
Design: Design 23

ISBN 1 84403 342 2
EAN 9781844033423

To Mike Channing, Varley Barrington-Cook, Doug Sinclair, Paul Sutton and Den Golding who were there with me during the schooboy years. To Simon Lamdin who was there when psychedelia hit the English South Coast in the mid-'70s. To David Chapman, Julie-Anne Fraser, Pete Hiscox, 'Mad' Pete Polynyk, Sharon Barrett, Sue Hall, Vanessa Clarke, Chris Fraser, Andy Channing, Mick Tarrant from Armadillo Records, all there for Bournemouth's invigorating punk and post-punk era. To Martin Mitchell, Sandra and Trevor for those hairy trips from Pontypridd to Cardiff's Top Rank during that late '70s Welsh sabbatical. To Fiona Bleach, Trevor King, Robin Cremer, Joe Cole and Sarah Wilford for those let's do it ourselves years. And to Peter Doggett, Lorne Murdoch, John Reed, Pat Gilbert, Andy Davis, Andy Neill, Zulema Gonzalez and all the others for the past couple of decades in London.

RIP: Nude At 70, The Animal Haircuts (Wink!), Vast Goat, Dub Sheep, The Dogloo Arts Group, The Grizzelders (also featuring Liam 'Toe Rag' Watson, Ivor 'Freakbeat' Trueman, Lesley 'Silverfish' Rankin and drummer Angie), Breadwinner.

Still on the road: Pixiphone, Pork Sword.

CONTENTS

INTRODUCTION

No, I wasn't there. Not unless you're talking about the night a baying crowd of Siouxsie And The Banshees fans forced Nico off stage with a chorus of boos and a shower of beer glasses. Or that golden day at the inaugural WOMAD Festival when the thundering sound of The Drummers Of Burundi reduced the rock acts present to a virtual sideshow. Or the night Kurt Cobain bade farewell to his British audience at a typically mud-splattered Reading Festival in 1992. But, with one or two exceptions, I wish I had been (and at the Melanie show, especially).

I Was There lifts the lid on a century's worth of classic performances, legendary in-concert moments, included here for their historical significance, era-defining importance, or simply their you-just-had-to-be-there rep. Through a combination of on-the-spot reportage, new research and personal recollections from musicians and critics, photographers and the fans themselves, this book allows you to relive those moments vicariously. Which, in the case of the Rolling Stones' tragic appearance at the Altamont Festival, is no doubt the preferred way to experience it.

On a personal note I, too, had a Rolling Stones performance ruined after misguidedly accepting a few swigs from a biker's plastic beaker at Knebworth during that sweltering summer of '76. By the time the band came on, ungraciously late, Jagger's characteristic finger-pointing had miraculously metamorphosed into something akin to Thor setting the sky ablaze. That's virtually my only memory from the show. But then obliteration of some form or another is often a significant part of the concert experience. Lost in the crowd. Lost in music, preferably at ear-crunching volume. In liquor or some other mind-changing substance. Lost in moments that have since become cornerstones of popular music history.

Had these selections been based on my own bulging bag of old ticket stubs, *I Was There* would have included Roxy Music with Eno in spring 1973, the Stones with Mick Taylor later that year, Captain Beefheart And His Magic Band in 1975, Hot Tuna at the Roundhouse in '76, any number of punk-era shows from the late 70s (The Slits, This Heat and Joy Division for starters), Sonic Youth, Radiohead, Acid Mothers Temple, maybe even the time I was smuggled into a "journos not welcome" Spice Girls performance at the Albert Hall. And, as you'll discover as you begin turning the pages of this book, there really is no such thing as a definitive list. So if your favourite show isn't here, you're by no means alone...

Mark Paytress, London, April 2005

American Roots

FROM THE MUSIC-HALL STAGES OF EAST LONDON TO THE GLITTERING PALACES OF HOLLYWOOD, POPULAR MUSIC FLOURISHED DURING THE EARLY DECADES OF THE 20TH CENTURY. BUT OUR JOURNEY BEGINS ON A MAKESHIFT STAGE IN A SMALL COMMUNITY IN GREENWOOD, MISSISSIPPI. THAT'S WHERE ROBERT JOHNSON, ON WHOSE SHOULDERS RESTS VIRTUALLY A CENTURY'S WORTH OF ROCK'N'ROLL MYTHOLOGY, PERFORMED HIS LAST, FATEFUL CONCERT BEFORE SUCCUMBING TO A FATAL DOSE OF STRYCHNINE.

THE HELLHOUND OF TRAGEDY MIGHT SEEM TO HAVE FOLLOWED SOME OF THE MOST GIFTED PERFORMERS IN POPULAR MUSIC EVER SINCE, BUT THERE'S ANOTHER, UNTOLD STORY, THE SHEER EXHILARATION OF CONCERTGOING, OF THE TRANSFIXED GAZE, OF SIMPLY BEING ABLE TO SAY, "I WAS THERE". AND ONCE ALAN FREED AND HIS CONTROVERSIAL MOONDOG SHOWS HAD INTRODUCED THE PHRASE ROCK'N'ROLL INTO POPULAR PARLANCE, THE ROLE PLAYED BY THE AUDIENCE HAS BEEN EVERY BIT AS CRUCIAL AS THAT OF THE PERFORMERS. THAT'S HOW ROCK'N'ROLL FORCED ITS WAY INTO THE SPOTLIGHT, BY THE SHEER WEIGHT OF NUMBERS WHO'D ATTENDED FREED'S SHOWS, AND THE UNPRECEDENTED MILLIONS WHO TUNED IN WHEN ELVIS PRESLEY MADE HIS FIRST APPEARANCES ON US TELEVISION. THE ELDERS MIGHT HAVE SNIFFED AT THE SEXUAL, AND POTENTIALLY REVOLUTIONARY UNDERTONES INHERENT IN THE NEW MUSIC, BUT HERE AT LAST WAS A GENUINELY POPULAR CULTURE, ENDORSED BY THE MASSES AND MET BY A SEEMINGLY NON-STOP FLOW OF HARD-UP HEROES ARMED SIMPLY WITH ATTITUDE AND A GUITAR.

ROBERT JOHNSON
THREE FORKS, GREENWOOD, MISSISSIPPI, JULY 1938

Given that it took place in what was little more than a private house, with whisky, rye and women in apparently abundant supply, eyewitness accounts of Robert Johnson's last stand at Three Forks have always been in short supply. Probably the best account we have comes from that giant blues storyteller Sonny Boy Williamson, who claimed to have performed with the Delta blues legend that last fateful night.

Johnson's popularity in and around the Mississippi Delta region had grown during the mid-Thirties, when rumours began to spread that he had sold his soul to the devil at the crossroads of Highway 61 and Highway 49 on the outskirts of Clarkesdale. How else, audiences asked, could he play those lightning lead lines and rhythmic bass lines simultaneously, or sing 'Hellhound On My Trail' with such haunted passion?

By July 1938, Johnson's wandering had landed him in Greenwood, Mississippi. On Saturday nights, he would play a place known as Three Forks, where he flirted with a local woman. Whether Johnson knew it or not, her husband owned the house. According to Sonny Boy, when his colleague took a break from the session one Saturday, he was offered a bottle of whisky. An open bottle. Acutely aware of the rancour Johnson's liaison – which had apparently been going on for a couple of weeks – had created, the harmonica player promptly whipped the bottle away. "Don't never knock a bottle of whisky outta my hand," Johnson warned, and when he was offered a second bottle, he immediately accepted it.

But Sonny Boy was right. Almost as soon as Johnson began to sing again, he raced outside and was sick. The whisky had been laced with strychnine. Although the dose was not instantly fatal, Robert Johnson died a couple of weeks later, on 16 August 1938, unaware that the crossroads where his life met his work would become the defining myth of the 20th-century outlaw musician.

"Don't never knock a bottle of whisky outta my hand."
ROBERT JOHNSON

FROM SPIRITUALS TO SWING

CARNEGIE HALL, NEW YORK, 23 DECEMBER 1938

It was an unprecedented, hugely ambitious project: to bring together the various strands of black music, from tribal Africa to the plethora of styles that had emerged out of the African-American experience. As a damning indication of black culture's (lack of) status in contemporary America, this remarkable event almost fell through because the organizers were unable to find a commercial sponsor. Eventually, *New Masses*, the arts magazine of the American Communist Party, came forward to save the show.

There was no such lack of interest on the part of New York's curious, overwhelmingly middle-class audience, who clapped enthusiastically if politely at the array of largely unsung talent on display. It was an extraordinary night, and the fact that it took place at all was largely down to John Hammond, Columbia Records' intrepid talent scout and the man responsible for unearthing Billie Holiday and Count Basie. With his magnificent ear and his historian's instinct for preservation, Hammond assembled a repertoire that showcased rural blues (Sonny Terry and Bull City Red) and gospel (Sister Rosetta Tharpe), boogie woogie (Albert Ammons) and big band swing (The Count Basie Orchestra), and plenty else besides. In fact, he kicked off the night himself, playing field recordings from Africa in the absence of funds to bring musicians across the Atlantic.

Another absentee was Robert Johnson, who Hammond had originally earmarked for the rural blues part of the show. The blues legend's death just four months earlier perhaps stole a march on the night's place in history. But even without Johnson – who was replaced by Big Bill Broonzy – From Spirituals To Swing remains a landmark concert in the development of popular music.

The extraordinary Sister Rosetta Tharpe, gospel-singing goddess from Arkansas.

Left: 'King Of Swing' Artie Shaw drops by at rehearsals for the Spirituals To Swing show, 22 December 1938. With him is conductor and jazz bandleader Paul Whiteman.

Below left: Big Bill Broonzy was joined by boogie-woogie piano legend Albert Ammons.

Opposite: Sister Rosetta Tharpe joins house bandleader Count Basie for a photo op during rehearsals for the legendary Carnegie Hall show.

From Spirituals to Swing, Carnegie Hall, New York, 1938

THE MOONDOG CORONATION BALL

CLEVELAND ARENA, CLEVELAND, OHIO, 21 MARCH 1952

If anyone deserves to be called the father of rock'n'roll, that person is Alan Freed. A DJ for a local radio station, WJW, in Cleveland, Ohio, Freed began spinning the latest rhythm'n'blues (or "race") records in summer 1951. In a bid to reach a wider, white audience, he gave the music a new name – rock'n'roll – and rechristened his show Moondog's Rock'n'Roll Party.

Freed used his programme to publicize the first ever rock'n'roll concert, which he put together in conjunction with two local businessmen. Hiring the vast Cleveland Arena, he booked "sensational stars" such as The Dominoes, together with the lesser known Tiny Grimes And The Rockin' Highlanders, Varetta Dillard and Danny Cobb. However, the real star of the show was the audience, all 25,000 of them who created havoc as the 10,000-seater venue struggled to contain them. Windows and doors were destroyed, the police were called and the show was stopped. Rock'n'roll had its first headlines.

By the mid-Fifties, when rock'n'roll hit its peak, Freed's rock'n'roll shows had become commonplace. Shortly after he had started working for WINS radio in New York, he organized the Rock'n'Roll Jubilee Ball – the first of many shows in the city – at St Nicholas Arena in Harlem on 14–15 January 1955. By now, the bill was strictly first-rate, with Clyde McPhatter And The Drifters, The Harptones, The Moonglows, The Clovers, Big Joe Turner and Fats Domino among those on the receiving end of the DJ's constant cries to "Go, Man, Go!"

Freed's best-known shows – and with his oddly avuncular face staring down from each and every poster, Freed made sure he was the star of the show – were the regular revues he put on at the Paramount in Brooklyn, usually at Easter, Labor Day and Christmas. These continued until the late Fifties, when the DJ was brought down by a series of scandals, some no doubt deliberate attempts to quell his activities, which were regarded as a potential threat to the moral health of the nation.

Mr Rock'n'Roll DJ Alan Freed exhorts the audience to "Go, man, go!" at a Cleveland WJW show (also pictured page 16) and (previous page) crowds at the Paramount Theatre, Brooklyn, New York, Easter 1955.

Windows and doors were destroyed, the police were called and rock'n'roll had its first headlines.

The Moondog Coronation Ball, Cleveland, 1952

CHARLIE PARKER QUINTET
MASSEY HALL, TORONTO, 15 MAY 1953

"The entire audience rose as one and swayed with closed eyes."
ALAIN PRESENCER

The sign outside couldn't have been more understated: "Jazz Concert Tonight". History, though, views the night quite differently. It was, legend has it, "The Greatest Jazz Concert Ever".

By 1953, be-bop king Charlie Parker was past his creative best, and in such poor health that he would be dead within two years. He had even begun turning up for concerts without his trusty Selmer sax; on this occasion, a local music shop loaned him an alto – a plastic one. Even on the night, Parker seemed easily distracted, showing more interest in the Rocky Marciano–Joe Walcott heavyweight fight that was being broadcast on a television backstage. However, when he did make it onto the stage, as part of the mightiest jazz quintet ever assembled in one place, Parker still had it.

The line-up was made in be-bop heaven: booze-sozzled pianist Bud Powell, the mighty Charlie Mingus on bass, fat-cheeked Dizzy Gillespie on trumpet, hard-hitting drummer Max Roach, and of course Parker on plastic alto. However, according to poet/musician Alain Presencer, then a 14-year-old aspiring jazz buff, the first half of the show – played out to a hall barely a quarter full – was dull, with Parker and Gillespie rarely on the stage, and Powell's piano playing all over the place.

The second half was different altogether. The show exploded with a version of 'Perdido', featuring Parker and Gillespie trading immaculate solos. A standing ovation immediately followed. Even Bud Powell seemed to pull himself together, especially for 'All The Things You Are', and on mellifluous versions of 'Salt Peanuts' and 'Wee' all five musicians worked together as one.

The night's *pièce de résistance*, though, was the final number, 'Night In Tunisia'. As Charlie Parker took off on what was one of his last truly great solos, Presencer recalled: "The entire audience rose as one and swayed with closed eyes. To this day I can remember the tears that cascaded down my cheeks as Parker's tortured voice screamed and wailed each bloody phrase into shapes of liquid noise."

Previous page: "And on borrowed plastic Grafton alto sax . . . Charlie Parker!"

Left: four of the quintet mingle with the supporting musicians – Charlie Mingus (back to photographer), Dizzy Gillespie (trumpet), Max Roach (drums) and out front, Charlie Parker.

Below left: Erratic piano genius Bud Powell. Below right: Be-bopping Max Roach, Dizzy Gillespie and Charlie Parker.

Charlie Parker Quintet, Massey Hall, Toronto, 1953

He was The Cry Guy, The Nabob of Sob, The Million Dollar Teardrop, the missing link between Frank Sinatra and Elvis Presley. With his hearing aid clearly visible below his Brylcreemed hair, Ray was a ham heartbreaker, a compelling balladeer whose near punkish amateurism elicited the first genuine screams from the new generation of post-war teenagers. In April 1955, just as his latest sob story, 'If You Believe', was enjoying chart success, he flew into Britain to create more heart-tugging havoc.

"The seat next to me was empty because my friend hadn't turned up," remembers Erika Lewis, then a schoolgirl Johnnie fan. So when he started to sing 'Walking My Baby Back Home', he came

JOHNNIE RAY
LONDON PALLADIUM, LONDON APRIL, 1955

right up beside me and I was soooo embarrassed! But very excited. He was a really big star then."

And Johnnie Ray wasn't just for the girls. "He generated more intensity than any performer I ever saw in my life, Judy Garland excepted," remembered Nic Cohn in *Awopbopaloobop Alopbamboom*, his classic history of rock'n'roll.

Johnnie Ray, London Palladium, 1955

Above: Johnnie Ray is greeted by fans, gathered outside the London Palladium. His hearing aid is clearly visible.

Left: A fan who has come to greet Johnnie Ray at the airport is rewarded with a kiss.

Johnnie Ray, London Palladium, 1955

"I'm a sort of human spaniel. People come to see what I'm like. I make them feel. I exhaust them. I destroy them." JOHNNIE RAY

From Skiffle To Sophistication

THE FIRST FLOURISH OF ROCK'N'ROLL HAD FIRMLY

PLACED YOUTH ON THE AGENDA AS A CULTURAL FORCE. SCOUTS AND CYCLING CLUBS WERE NO LONGER THE SOLE OPTIONS. NOW THERE WAS SKIFFLE, A STREET CORNER LAUNCH-PAD TOWARDS POP FAME, A DO-IT-YOURSELF FUSION OF FOLK SONG, ROCK'N'ROLL AND HIT PARADE BALLADRY. AMONG THE THOUSANDS OF TEENAGERS INSPIRED INTO ACTION WAS THE YOUNG JOHN LENNON, WHOSE QUARRY MEN GROUP WERE A REGULAR ATTRACTION AT STREET PARTIES AND GARDEN FETES.

AS LENNON AND HIS WARTIME GENERATION CAME OF AGE, THEIR HEROES STARTED TO LOSE THEIR LUSTRE. JERRY LEE LEWIS WAS HOUNDED OUT OF BRITAIN WHEN THE MORALITY OF THE DEEP SOUTH WAS DEEMED INCOMPATIBLE WITH THAT OF CONTEMPORARY BRITAIN. BUDDY HOLLY HOPPED ONTO A PRIVATE PLANE SHORTLY AFTER A GIG, AND FLEW RIGHT OFF INTO ROCK'N'ROLL HEAVEN. MEANWHILE, ELVIS PRESLEY HAD BEEN HIJACKED BY HOLLYWOOD AND THE US ARMY. ONLY VINCE TAYLOR, A FABULOUSLY CULTISH ROCK'N'ROLL RENEGADE WHO FOUND AN EAGER MARKET FOR HIS DERANGED ON-STAGE ANTICS IN FRANCE, CONTINUED TO CARRY THE TORCH OF TEDDY BOY DANGER.

THE ROCK'N'ROLL DREAM WAS FAST FADING, BUT IT HAD CHANGED THE LANDSCAPE FOREVER, AS THE SUCCESS OF LEONARD BERNSTEIN'S *WEST SIDE STORY* – *ROMEO AND JULIET* WITH ADDED TEENAGE DELINQUENCY – PROVED. AND THERE WERE OTHER STRANDS EMERGING, TOO, THAT WOULD SOON RE-ENERGIZE POPULAR MUSIC. JAMES BROWN WAS TAKING THE ART OF SHOWMANSHIP TO NEW LEVELS, WITH EVERYONE FROM MICK JAGGER AND TINA TURNER DOWNWARDS EAGERLY TAKING NOTES. AND IN AN ERA OF MILD MUSICAL CONSERVATISM, IT WAS LEFT TO JAZZ MAESTRO MILES DAVIS TO CONTINUE PUSHING THE BARRIERS FORWARD, WHICH IN TURN HELPED INSPIRE ROCK'S COMING OF AGE LATER IN THE DECADE.

ELVIS PRESLEY
THE MILTON BERLE SHOW, 3 APRIL AND 5 JUNE 1956

'Heartbreak Hotel', a huge hit early in 1956, proved traumatic enough, but it wasn't until the middle of the year that the thrillingly untamed newcomer with the strange name and the even stranger voice truly waltzed into controversy. Taking the tempo right down on his latest song, 'Hound Dog', Elvis Presley began to swivel his hips in an almost unconscious display of bump'n'grind – and thus, in front of millions, was born "Elvis The Pelvis".

The occasion was Presley's second appearance on *The Milton Berle Show*, a light entertainment programme presented by the man once known as "Mister Television". On this particular night, the small-screen presenter was caught off guard. Presley's loose limbs prompted a nationwide panic in the press, in factories and offices and, of course, the church. "Beware Elvis Presley," warned one religious broadsheet. "Vulgar and animalistic," screamed the press. It was as if all the nation's anxieties about teenage delinquency and, worse still, teen sexuality had fallen on Presley's shoulders.

"I don't feel I'm doing anything wrong," Elvis countered in one televised phone-in shortly after the broadcast, but that didn't stop radio stations from organizing week-long record-smashing sessions, or the police from surreptitiously filming his performances with a view to prosecuting him.

It was all a far cry from Presley's first appearance on Berle's show back in April when, with his rock'n'roll trio, he performed 'Shake, Rattle And Roll', 'Blue Suede Shoes' and his recent chart-topping hit 'Heartbreak Hotel' with barely a squeak from the public. Broadcast from the deck of the USS *Hancock*, and featuring a skit where the presenter pretended to be Elvis's long-lost brother, it couldn't have been more wholesome.

After the incendiary second show, though, the backlash only served to intensify interest in the young singer. By the time Elvis Presley stepped up to the microphone for the first of three appearances on the prestigious *Ed Sullivan Show*, a reported 52 million Americans – one in three of the population – eagerly tuned in to catch the winds of change.

Elvis Presley, The Milton Berle Show, 1956

NAT 'KING' COLE
MUNICIPAL AUDITORIUM, BIRMINGHAM, ALABAMA, 10 APRIL 1956

> ## "I just came here to entertain. That's what I thought they wanted."
> ### NAT 'KING' COLE

By the mid-Fifties, Nat 'King' Cole was the most successful black American entertainer in the world. Having established his reputation as a piano-playing singer with the Nat 'King' Cole Trio during the Forties, he'd released a string of sumptuous, million-selling ballads such as 'Nature Boy' and 'Mona Lisa'. Known as "the man with the velvet voice" (not forgetting the charming smile and formal eveningwear), Cole was so popular with (white) Middle America that, early in 1957, he was about to be given his own television series.

However, the singer's willingness to perform to segregated audiences, despite the Supreme Court's decision in 1954 that such a practice was "unconstitutional", earned him much criticism from within the black community. "I'm just an entertainer," Cole countered, unwilling to set himself up as a political crusader. But with the civil rights movement gaining in strength during the decade, Cole's stance did seem increasingly out of step with the times. Then, one dark night in Birmingham, Alabama, in America's Deep South, Cole – a gentle man who had already suffered racial hatred when he moved into an affluent area of Los Angeles – was rudely awakened to the depravity of the situation.

Cole had been booked to play two separate shows, one at 8pm to an all-white crowd, followed by a midnight set to a black audience. Whispers of potential trouble had prompted an added police presence around the Municipal Auditorium stage during the first show, and the authorities' worst fears were realized when, midway through the

second number, 'Little Girl', five men thundered down the aisles towards the stage. One struck the singer, knocking him down onto the piano stool, which broke on impact. Another had hold of Cole's foot before eight policemen dragged the assailants off the stage.

While this was going on, the 18-piece Ted Heath Orchestra, which had flown in from England to play with Cole, launched into a patriotic 'My Country 'Tis Of Thee'. Backstage, Cole was bruised and shaken. "I'm just befuddled," he said. Comedian Gary Morton ran out and told the audience that the singer was unable to continue with the show. Amid the tumult, one lone voice cried out "We want to apologize", prompting Cole to change his mind. He re-emerged to a lengthy ovation.

After a short lay-off, Nat 'King' Cole rejoined the tour four nights later, though the incident had changed him. "I love showbiz," he told a friend, "but I don't want to die for it." He promptly joined the NAACP civil rights group and never played to a segregated audience again. His white supremacist attackers, who it was later discovered had intended to kidnap the singer, were subsequently prosecuted. Segregation seemed even more unjust and antiquated after this concert, though in truth the battle against racism was just beginning.

Top left: The shocked singer hides behind the curtain while police escort his assailants from the building and into custody.
Right: Nat 'King' Cole reconsidered his decision to play to segregated audiences in the wake of the attack.

"People say I'm an alcoholic, a dope addict, a nympho and a kleptomaniac. Well, it's all true." That's how Billie Holiday began her autobiography, published in August 1956, a traumatic tale of hard knocks, mind-numbing highs and an insatiable desire to sing. Three months later, the audience at New York's prestigious Carnegie Hall lived vicariously for a night while Billie stood up and sang the soundtrack to her troubled existence. As if to reinforce the inseparability of art and life, her roughly hewn set was interspersed by four lengthy extracts from the book, read by critic Gilbert Millstein.

Though probably a decade past her peak, Billie Holiday was deadly serious about this show, beginning rehearsals for the book/concert tie-in as early as the spring. She was back working with a small band, and the set was largely made up of her own material. Better still, she'd managed to put at least some of her problems behind her – including a drug-related court case at the start of the year – and much of the old intensity was back.

Reviewing the show, *Down Beat*'s Nat Hentoff called her "the best jazz singer alive". The *New York Times* admitted that, while often "erratic", at Carnegie Hall, Holiday "sang with assurance", further citing "her rough, throaty croon and her expressive dips, lifts and dolorously twisted notes". Gilbert Millstein, who shared the stage with her, was equally impressed. "It was utterly superb," he declared. "She was thoroughly professional, alert, took her cues perfectly, made not a single mistake."

At last, it seemed, Billie Holiday was receiving her due. Even Hollywood had begun sniffing round in the wake of the book and the Carnegie concerts, but, unlike the star, they still had a lot to learn. It was said that Lana Turner, an actress with a fine Hollywood pedigree and not without her own personal problems, had been earmarked to play the singer. Lana Turner was white.

Opposite: The inimitable Billie Holiday in 1956, erratic but still singing with remarkable assurance said the critics.

Right: Billie Holiday performed at Carnegie Hall on several occasions. Here she is at the venue in 1946.

QUARRY MEN
St Peter's Church Fete, Woolton, Liverpool
6 July 1957

More commonly known as "The Day John Met Paul", 6 July 1957 was a perfectly ordinary English summer's day. The scent of school holidays was in the air and a whiff of medieval tradition, too, as a loud, lively and gaily clad procession of merrymakers made its way towards the village fete in Woolton, three miles north-east of Liverpool city centre. There were neatly turned-out scouts and guides, excitable schoolchildren in a variety of home-made costumes and the obligatory Morris dancers.

At around 4.15pm, in a field at the back of St Peter's Church, the crowd milling around the various stalls were alerted to an "eruption of noise". At least that was the impression of John Lennon's aunt and *de facto* mother Aunt Mimi, who looked up and saw the young man she had brought up since he'd been a small boy shaking his guitar and singing, "Oh, Mimi's coming down the path…"

Even more surprised to see the young rock'n'roll fanatic fronting a ragged skiffle band on a makeshift stage was schoolboy Paul McCartney, at 15, two years Lennon's junior, but no less obsessed with the greasy sounds of young America.

The Quarry Men raced through skiffle standards such as 'Cumberland Gap', 'Puttin' On The Style' and 'Maggie Mae' (later covered by The Beatles on *Let It Be*), then did it all over again for a second set at 5.45pm. In readiness for a third, evening session, the group reconvened for a few beers in the scouts' hut. That's where Paul McCartney, sporting a slicked-back DA (duck's arse) hairstyle, drainpipe trousers and a flashy white sports jacket, was introduced to Lennon by a mutual friend, Ivan Vaughn. Lennon's initial disinterest apparently melted when McCartney picked up a guitar, tuned it and then launched into Gene Vincent's 'Be Bop A-Lula' and a medley of Little Richard songs. "That's how it started really," McCartney remembered at the height of Beatlemania.

Just weeks before the garden fete in Woolton, the Quarry Men played another open-air concert in Liverpool's Roseberry Street – where this historic photograph was taken.

Quarry Men, Woolton, Liverpool, 1957

WEST SIDE STORY
WINTER GARDEN THEATER, NEW YORK, 26 SEPTEMBER 1957

A latter-day *Romeo and Juliet* played out on the mean streets of New York's Lower East Side, *West Side Story* dramatized the world of the teenage ghetto gangs for theatregoers of Middle America. Brilliantly scored by Leonard Bernstein, with lyrics by Stephen Sondheim, this hugely successful musical premiered – before running for 732 shows on Broadway, over 1,000 in London's West End and going international with the Hollywood blockbuster in 1961 – at precisely the moment that rock'n'roll began to lose its way.

Taking the panic concerning "juvenile delinquency" as its theme, *West Side Story* elevated the art of the American musical, its undercurrents of anti-racism and liberal attitude towards poverty providing a healthy riposte to the rampant McCarthyism and conservative politics of the era. Best of all, though, was the music itself – 'Maria', 'I Feel Pretty', 'Somewhere' and 'Tonight' being among the finest quartet of songs written for any single project in the era of mass-produced popular music.

Left: Larry Kent (Tony) and Carol Lawrence (Maria) steal a romantic moment at the New York premiere of Bernstein's stunning, Shakespeare-inspired tale of teenage delinquency

Opposite: The Jets and The Sharks battle it out.

West Side Story, New York, 1957

JERRY LEE LEWIS

JERRY MAY HAVE TO CUT HIS TOUR

When the reportedly lewd and lascivious Jerry Lee Lewis rolled into London in May 1958, he was the hottest contender to Elvis Presley in the King of Rock'n'Roll stakes. Within a week, he had been bundled out of the country in disgrace, his young wife Myra in tow. The crowds, who could hardly wait to whoop "Goodness! Gracious! Great balls of fire!" back at their hero, greeted him instead with angry cries of "Go home, baby snatcher!", "Kiddy thief!" and – so one paper reported – "Get home, you crumb!"

Controversy had dogged Jerry Lee Lewis right from the start. A man of deep contradictions, whose Pentecostal upbringing had been rudely interrupted by a sudden calling to play "the devil's music", he had become an anti-hero in the United States the previous summer with the sexually charged 'Whole Lotta Shakin' Goin' On'. His records blacklisted by many radio stations, Jerry Lee's stage shows – where he would kick away his stool, play piano with his feet, let his long hair dangle over his eyes and sometimes trash his instrument completely – seemed to epitomize everything that was repellent about rock'n'roll.

However, the stick used to beat the visiting rocker in Britain was the scandal of Jerry Lee's private life. Within hours of his arrival at London Airport on 22 May, the press – mindful of his reputation – was outraged that the 22-year-old singer was already on wife number three who, worse still, was just 15. Within days, it was further revealed that Jerry Lee was a bigamist twice over, and that his bride Myra Gale was actually just 13 and the daughter of Jerry Lee's cousin.

The tour was meant to last more than a month, but with the newspapers whipping up the controversy – "Get out, Lewis!" advised the *Daily Sketch* – Jerry Lee managed just three concerts,

all in and around the London area. Despite good ticket sales, none was more than half full, and many in the audience had come to barrack the disgraced US star. Looking every inch the deviant rock'n'roller, in his custard-coloured suit with black sequined braiding and ribbon tie, Jerry Lee Lewis delivered his 25-minute set to receptions that ranged from muted to downright hostile. Cliff Richard felt comfortable enough to be photographed with the pianist backstage at the Kilburn State Empire, but by the time the tour hit the Tooting Granada on Monday 26 May, the antipathy between star and audience was mutual. "Yo' all seem awful quiet out there," taunted Jerry Lee. "Ah'm alive. I sho' hope yo' all ain't half as dead as yo' sound."

The Rank Organization, which had booked the tour, cancelled the rest of the dates in order to prevent "irreparable harm to British showbusiness". By Tuesday evening, Jerry Lee Lewis and his child bride were on their way home – to face further controversy.

> **"Everybody thinks I am a ladies' man and a bad boy, but I am not. I am a good boy and I want everyone to know that." JERRY LEE LEWIS TO THE *DAILY EXPRESS*, MAY 1958**

BUDDY HOLLY
SURF BALLROOM, CLEAR LAKE, IOWA, 2 FEBRUARY 1959

Buddy Holly's first flush of success was over. Having struck big with 'That'll Be The Day', which topped the US charts in 1957, his hits had begun to dry up just as America's initial love affair with rock'n'roll seemed to be on the wane.

By the time he embarked on a three-week package tour of the American midwest, with fellow hitmakers Richie Valens, The Big Bopper, Dion And The Belmonts and the little-known Frankie Sardo, Holly had also split from his backing band, The Crickets. To make matters worse, the tour bus had proved woefully inadequate, and the guerrilla-like raids on small and medium-sized towns in a nondescript landscape left Buddy Holly a mildly depressed man.

"It's disgusting," he told his wife Maria in a phone call on the night of the Clear Lake show. But the show had to go on, and once Valens had set things up with 'La Bamba', and The Big Bopper had everyone on their feet for 'Chantilly Lace', the man in the distinctive black glasses, crumpled suit and bow-tie ambled on stage alone with his electric guitar. Typically, he said few words to the crowd, and instead launched into 'Gotta Travel On', a country song soon to be a hit for Billy Grammer.

After his backing band – including a young Waylon Jennings – joined him, Holly took off on a crowd-pleasing run of hits, songs such as 'Peggy Sue', 'Heartbeat', 'Rave On', 'Everyday' and of course 'That'll Be The Day'. The audience of around 1,500 watched avidly as Holly pivoted his neck in time to his infectious, cleverly worked material.

By midnight the concert was over, and thoughts turned towards the gruelling 400-mile trip to the next stop in Minnesota. But, on this night, Buddy Holly was relaxed, almost pleased with himself. Determined to enjoy what was left of the Winter Dance Party tour, he'd made arrangements to fly ahead in a private plane. After much jostling for places, he was accompanied by the tour's other big stars, Richie Valens and The Big Bopper. Shortly after the plane left the ground at nearby Mason City, at 12.30am, it came down in a cornfield just five miles from Clear Lake. Years later, Don McLean's 'American Pie' paid tribute to the tragic loss, calling it "the day the music died".

The legendary Buddy Holly, killed in a plane crash shortly after the Surf Ballroom show.

The Miles Davis Quintet with Gil Evans

At the outset of the 1960s Miles Davis was the *enfant terrible* of the jazz world, who offended traditionalists with his giant stylistic steps while delighting thrill-seekers eager to embrace an unknowable new world. The embodiment of the cool black hipster, young, defiant and abundantly gifted, Davis was already something of an icon. At the beginning of 1961, *Ebony* magazine lauded him as "The evil genius of jazz". A few months later, *Gentleman's Quarterly* adopted him as their "Fashion personality for the month of May". The man with the horn, it seemed, could do no wrong.

However, with the departure of John Coltrane from his sextet in 1960, Miles entered a period of mild musical confusion that would last for the next few years, a difficult era punctuated by this milestone concert subsequently described by Miles's biographer Ian Carr as "one of the great performances in jazz history". That was, in part, due to the unprecedented pairing of Miles Davis's quintet with arranger Gil Evans and his orchestra.

Although on paper it was an unlikely pairing, the notoriously difficult-to-please Davis had much respect for the cultured arranger. Evans was, remembered the trumpeter, "this tall, thin, white guy from Canada who was hipper than hip". Although they

> **"Although he has often been charged with treating his audiences disdainfully, he not only smiled on a couple of occasions but acknowledged applause with a quick glance over the footlights and a slight nod of the head."**
>
> **JOHN WILSON, *NEW YORK TIMES***

had collaborated in the studio many times since the late 1940s, from *The Birth Of The Cool* to more recent productions such as *Porgy And Bess* and *Sketches Of Spain*, they had never performed together on stage before until the Carnegie concert.

Suitably inspired, Miles Davis reached new heights of sophistication that evening, with one of many highlights being the first live outing for the lengthy 'Concierto De Aranjuez', the centrepiece from *Sketches Of Spain*. "He played with tremendous fire and spirit, soaring off into high-note runs with confidence and precision," wrote John Wilson in the *New York Times*, "building lines bristling with searing emotion and yet retaining all the warmest, singing elements of his gentler side."

The Miles Davis Quintet, featuring tenor sax man Hank Mobley in particularly fine form, was by no means upstaged by the orchestra. In fact, the only threat of that came from drummer Max Roach, who was in the audience. Midway through 'Someday My Prince Will Come', Roach, who had doubts about the fund-raising affair, held up a placard that read: "AFRICA FOR THE AFRICANS! FREEDOM NOW!" Miles, normally a model of stoicism on stage, walked off. After a difficult few moments, he returned, his playing shot through with more intensity than ever.

Vince Taylor And The Playboys
Festival du Rock, Palais des Sports, Paris, 18 November 1961

"As soon as I get on stage," Vince Taylor once said, "I go out of myself, I lose control. Often I lose consciousness. Afterwards, I become myself again."

Born in west London, raised in the United States, Vince Taylor was the black-clad demon of rock'n'roll. "Wilder than a Neanderthal man," claimed one disapproving newspaper at the time. "Bonkers!" recalled David Bowie, who used Taylor as the inspiration for his Ziggy Stardust character.

Responsible for one of the few bona fide classic British rock'n'roll singles, 'Brand New Cadillac', Taylor struggled to find a niche in London at the beginning of the 1960s. One trip to Paris changed all that. Booked to prop up the bill on a package show at the Olympia in July 1961, he was quickly rescheduled to headline after the promoter caught him in rehearsal. Starved of authentic rock'n'roll, Paris went wild for Taylor, a spectacular vision complete with a Joan of Arc medallion that swang furiously from his neck.

Matters got seriously out of hand when Taylor returned to the city in November 1961 to play the third Festival du Rock at the Palais des Sports. Even before he had whipped them into a frenzy with his on-stage dramatics involving leather, chains and some genuinely incendiary rock'n'roll riffs, the audience had torn up the place. Taylor's cult hero status in his new adopted country was assured.

Then things went decidedly weird. Months later, Taylor began preaching from the Bible, imagining himself to be Jesus Christ. Returning to London for a few months during the mid-Sixties, he delighted acolytes such as the young David Bowie with tales of buried treasures and world conspiracies. After a lengthy battle with drugs and alcohol, Vince Taylor died in 1991.

Below, left: Vince Taylor salvages something from the wreckage after fans riot at his November 1961 show in Paris.

Below: "Vince Taylor – Leper Messiah!"

"The guy was unbelievable." DAVID BOWIE

JAMES BROWN

APOLLO THEATRE, HARLEM, NEW YORK, 24 OCTOBER 1962

"This is without a doubt one of the most exciting albums ever recorded at a live performance and the producers and engineers have completely captured the James Brown personality, the James Brown sound, the James Brown feel. This is the James Brown show, the show which is breaking records everywhere it plays, this is a full package of pure delight."

For once the note on the back of the record sleeve almost underplays the delights within, but writer Hal Neely wasn't to

know that, over 40 years on, James Brown's *Live At The Apollo* album would be widely recognized as the greatest live record ever made. Across six monumental songs, plus a medley that strings together several others, Brown rarely pauses for breath, while his meticulously rehearsed backing singers (The Famous Flames) and band hit each and every cue. More crucial than all this is the remarkable dynamic that exists between performer and audience, which reaches such a pitch during the almost painfully

Left: The Godfather of soul in commanding form at the Apollo.

Above: The legend of James Brown soon spread around the world. Here, two Mali teenagers proudly show off their copy of the Apollo recordings.

drawn-out 'Lost Someone' that one wonders just why all that fuss was made about Beatlemania a year or so later.

Had James Brown's record company boss had his way, we would have had to rely on hearsay in assessing the greatness of Brown's week-long stint at New York's legendary black music concert hall. Despite the singer's pedigree – he had been playing over 300 shows a year since the mid-Fifties and had enjoyed many hits in the R&B and sometimes pop charts – King Records boss Syd Nathan regarded Brown foremost as a concert attraction who made singles as a sideline. Brown, who stumped up his own cash to record the show, proved him wrong. The resulting album hit number two in the US charts, where it spent over a year, and sealed Brown's reputation both at home and abroad.

What *James Brown Live At The Apollo* doesn't fully manage to convey is the frontman's legendary showmanship. From the insistent rhythm of the opening 'I Go Crazy' to the closing groove of 'Night Train', the remarkably paced set is packed with a dramatic, almost manic intensity that lends itself to the singer's repertoire of visual cues. Introducing himself with the words "You know I feel all right!", Brown, his suit sparkling under the lights and his hair piled up high, tilts back his head and closes his eyes, until each instrumental break provides the cue for the singer to spin or fall to his knees – and then he's back into the song. His voice, raw and impassioned, is, above all, what touched the soul of the 1,500-strong crowd on a cold night in Harlem's Apollo Theatre.

James Brown, Apollo Theatre, New York, 1962   45

England
Swings

IT WAS A WHILE BEFORE THE DECADE TRULY IGNITED, BUT WHEN IT DID, THERE WAS ABSOLUTELY NO TURNING BACK. AND AT ITS CORE WAS THE POP CONCERT. OR, MORE ACCURATELY, THE PHENOMENON OF BEATLEMANIA. THE BEATLES HAD BEEN SEIZED UPON BY AN AUDIENCE DESPERATE FOR SOMETHING THAT WOULD BANISH THE PROTRACTED PERIOD OF POST-WAR AUSTERITY. IN AMERICA, THEIR "INVASION" ROUGHLY COINCIDED WITH KENNEDY'S ASSASSINATION, AND IN MANY WAYS THEY BECAME THE TORCH-BEARERS FOR HIS YOUTHFUL AND, DOMESTICALLY AT LEAST, LIBERAL CRUSADE.

THE SEDATE, CLANDESTINE EVEN, CONCERTS OF THE EARLY 1960S WERE COMPLETELY ECLIPSED BY THE ENERGIES UNLEASHED BY THE BEAT GROUPS. THE BEATLES' APPEARANCES AT THE CAVERN, LIVERPOOL, HAD GIVEN LITTLE INDICATION OF THE MAGNITUDE OF THEIR SUBSEQUENT SUCCESS. LIKEWISE THE ROLLING STONES, LONDON'S RHYTHM'N'BLUES NOVITIATES, WHOSE 1963 RESIDENCY AT THE CRAWDADDY IN RICHMOND ONE NIGHT PROMPTED A SURPRISE VISIT FROM JOHN, PAUL, GEORGE AND RINGO. EVERYONE WANTED A BIT OF WHAT THE BEATLES HAD, AND JOHN, PAUL, GEORGE AND RINGO ALL KNEW IT.

BY THE TIME THE FAB FOUR HAD TRULY CONQUERED AMERICA WITH THEIR ENORMOUS SHEA STADIUM SHOW IN AUGUST 1965, THEIR COMPETITORS WERE ALREADY PULLING AT THE LEASH. AT THE MARQUEE IN LONDON, THE WHO DRESSED THEIR SOUND IN ART, VIOLENCE AND STREET STYLE. BALLADEERS SUCH AS PJ PROBY BEGAN TO GROW THEIR HAIR AND BECOME SUGGESTIVE TO THE POINT OF INDECENCY. AMERICA EXPORTED ITS OWN SOUNDS, NOTABLY THE DETROIT-BASED TAMLA-MOTOWN FOUNTAIN OF TALENT. AND, MOST CRUCIALLY INTELLECTUALS AND POP MUSICIANS BEGAN TO FRATERNIZE. AS A HARBINGER FOR WHAT WAS TO COME, THE INTERNATIONAL POETRY READING AT THE ALBERT HALL IN JUNE 1965 REMAINS A SIGNIFICANT LANDMARK. NO BEAT GROUPS PERFORMED THAT DAY, NOR DID MAN OF THE MOMENT BOB DYLAN. BUT THE EVENT CONFIRMED THAT THE AUDIENCES FOR POETRY AND POP WERE NOWHERE NEAR AS DISTINCT AS THEY HAD BEEN TWO YEARS EARLIER.

"We were performers in Liverpool, Hamburg and other dance halls and what we generated was fantastic. We played straight rock and there was nobody to touch us in Britain. As soon as we made it, the edges were knocked off. We sold out, you know."

John Lennon

THE BEATLES
THE CAVERN CLUB, MATHEW STREET, LIVERPOOL, 1961–1963

When The Beatles started playing lunchtime sessions at The Cavern, they were earning around a fiver a show. When they returned there for one last show on 3 August 1963, they were the most famous young men in Britain whose records were beginning to sell in millions. The Cavern era was the most dramatic in the band's history. In an intense, two-year spell, during which time they acquired drummer Ringo Starr and manager, Brian Epstein, and also managed to perfect their craft, The Beatles played The Cavern around 300 times.

"The atmosphere in The Cavern was like nothing else on earth," remembered Cynthia Lennon. "The entrance was tiny, the stairs leading into the cellar were narrow and uneven. The unsavoury aroma of damp and sweat pervaded even the most blocked-up of nostrils, a common complaint in Liverpool."

Opposite: John and Paul had over 300 opportunities to perfect their harmonies in a sweat-drenched cellar in Liverpool.

Left: John Lennon, in action at The Cavern.

Overleaf: The Cavern in the early '60s. "A claustrophobic but highly energetic ambience," remembers one lunchtime regular.

"When I was in the 6th form, studying for A-levels, once, or sometimes twice a week I used to get the Number 47 bus to Liverpool City Centre and go to the Picton Library to 'study' in the mornings. Then before going back to school at the end of Menlove Avenue in Woolton, I used to go to The Cavern for one of the famous lunchtime sessions.

"It was 2 shillings admission to see some of the best groups in the world playing during a two-hour session. At the time, to our untrained eyes and ears, there was little to choose between them in musical ability and enthusiasm. The atmosphere was the same whoever was playing – crowded, sweaty, smoky, and hardly much room to dance, unlike some of the other larger dance halls in Liverpool at the time. The low ceiling and packed audiences contributed to the claustrophobic but highly energetic ambience.

"Some of the groups playing quickly became household names. As well as The Beatles, The Cavern attracted The Searchers, Gerry And The Pacemakers and The Merseybeats. The local Liverpudlians' favourites were more likely to include Rory Storm And The Hurricanes, The Swinging Blue Jeans and my own favourites, The Big Three. Many talented but 'no-name' bands were on the bill as well.

"I remember the lunchtime audiences being almost entirely made up of locals and a large proportion of us were in some form of not very subtly disguised school uniform. Oh, and I don't remember any alcohol being served at lunchtime in the early days!"

Cavern Club regular

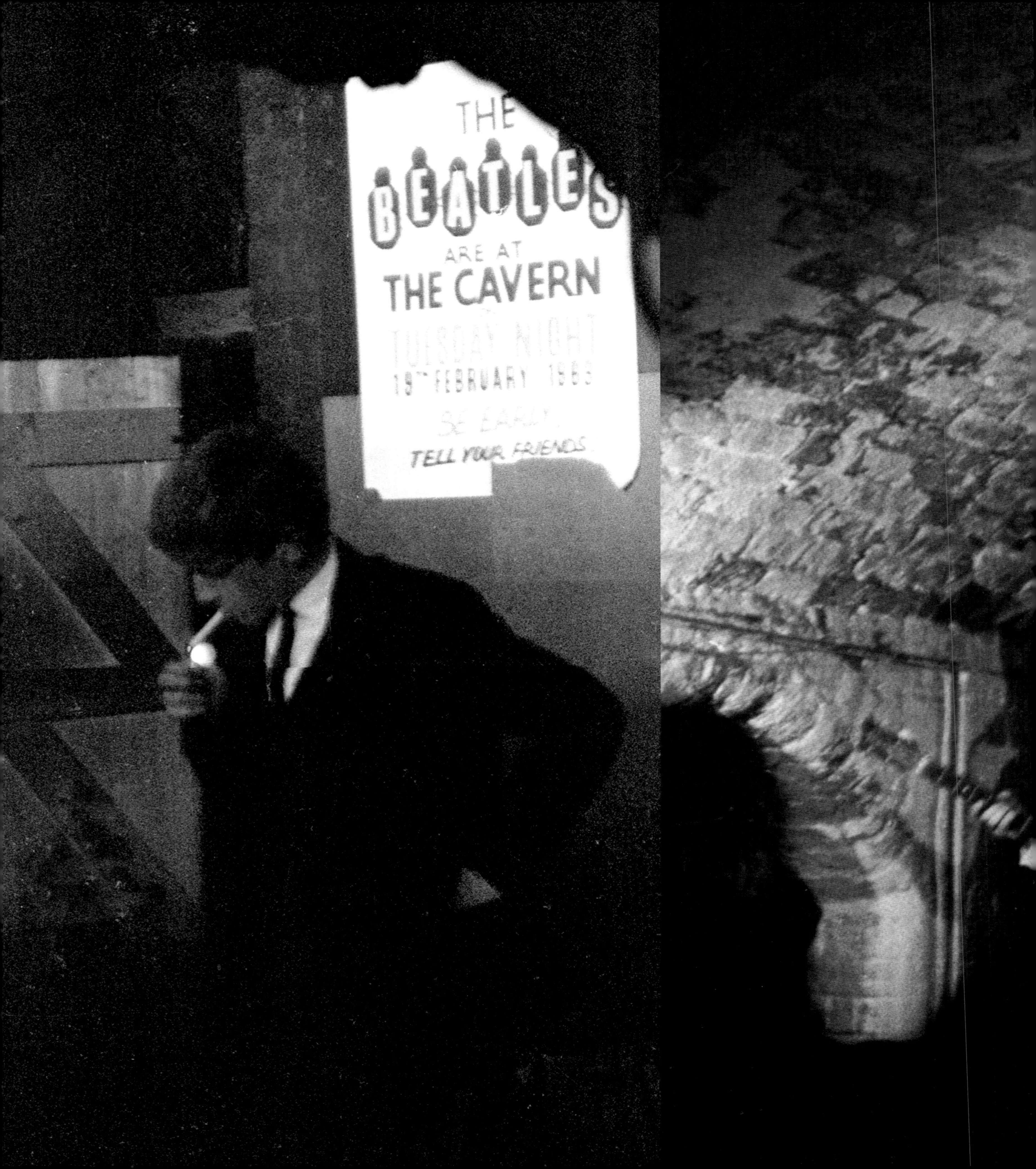
THE
BEATLES
ARE AT
THE CAVERN
TELL YOUR FRIENDS

THE ROLLING STONES
CRAWDADDY CLUB, RICHMOND, SURREY, 14 APRIL 1963

"Genuine R&B fanatics, they sing and play in a way that one would have expected more from a coloured US R&B team than a bunch of wild, exciting white boys who have the fans screaming."
NORMAN JOPLING, *RECORD MIRROR*

The weekend of 13–14 April 1963 was a significant one for the Rolling Stones. A couple of months into a Sunday night residency at the Station Hotel, in the suburbs of west London, they had already seen their audience grow from a couple of dozen to over 300 fans eager to catch the young, homegrown R&B group.

It began with the publication of a piece – the Stones' first press write-up – in the *Richmond and Twickenham Times*. "Rhythm and blues, gaining more popularity every week, is replacing 'traddypop' all over the country," wrote Barry May. "The deep, earthy sound produced at the hotel on Sunday evenings...gives all who hear it an irresistible urge to 'stand up and move'." Visually, too, he reckoned the Stones were distinctly cutting edge: "Hair worn Piltdown-style, brushed forward from the crown like The Beatles pop group."

According to May, the Crawdaddy was a dark room filled by a crowd notable for their "funny clothes". On 14 April, four young men in fittingly unconventional attire crept into the darkness. It was The Beatles, and they had dropped by to check out the competition. On the door to welcome them was Brian Jones's girlfriend Pat Andrews. "The Beatles' visit was pre-arranged," she says. Giorgio Gomelsky, the Stones' manager, had arranged it earlier in the day, travelling down to

nearby Twickenham where The Beatles had been filming.

"Brian asked me if I could put them somewhere where they could see," she adds. "It was one of the scariest moments of my life. I remember seeing this leather cap coming round the door. I think it was Ringo. They were all dressed in black leather, and I hid them in the shadows."

From the stage, bassist Bill Wyman looked out and thought, "Shit, that's The Beatles". He needn't have worried. "It was a real rave," reckoned George Harrison afterwards. "The audience shouted and screamed and danced on tables. They were doing a dance that no one had seen up till then, but we now all know as The Shake. The beat the Stones laid down was so solid it shook off the walls and seemed to move right inside your head. A great sound."

Above: The Stones' Sunday evening residency in Richmond, Surrey, marked a defining moment in the band's career.

Opposite: "Hair worn Piltdown-style, brushed forward from the crown like The Beatles pop group," described the local paper after its first, historic brush with Jagger and the boys.

That night, the audience witnessed a remarkable feat of baton passing.

JUDY GARLAND AND LIZA MINNELLI

LONDON PALLADIUM, LONDON, 8 NOVEMBER 1964

On 23 July 1964, Judy Garland, that grand dame of showbiz royalty, eclipsed even The Beatles at the London Palladium's *The Night Of A Hundred Stars*. Not even billed to perform, the screen legend more than lived up to her "World's Greatest Entertainer" reputation with an impromptu 'Over The Rainbow' that stole the show and made front-page news as "the comeback of the year".

No surprise, then, that before the year was out, Garland was back at her favourite venue in her favourite city for two sell-out shows. Only this time, she shared the stage with one of the few people in the world with the potential to upstage her...her 18-year-old daughter Liza Minnelli.

Mother and daughter had performed together before, on several occasions since 1956, though invariably Liza's role was little more than novelty value. At the Palladium, in November 1964, all that changed. By now, Judy's extraordinary career highs were fast being undermined by marriage, health and financial problems. Though the sign on her dressing room still read "The Legend", audiences never knew whether they were going to get bloated Judy or emaciated Judy, sparkling Judy or tired and emotional Judy. Liza, on the other hand, was fresh from finishing school and a triumphant stint off-Broadway. However, she did have to live up to being Judy Garland's daughter.

With that in mind, Liza Minnelli baulked initially at the suggestion of sharing the Palladium stage on equal terms with her mother, but Judy was having none of it, and promptly announced to the press that the joint show was going ahead. It was an immediate sell-out, and a second night at the intimate, opulent venue was hastily added.

What the audience witnessed, especially on the first night (Judy's voice suffered through a throat infection at the second show), was a remarkable feat of baton passing. Though no longer the bloated figure who had sung from the same stage four years earlier,

Judy looked tired in comparison to lithe, lively Liza. Sometimes when they traded lines on songs such as 'Get Happy', there was little difference between their remarkable voices. However, it was all too clear that one era was ending and another about to start – and no one could ignore the pathos as phrases such as "Watching my dreams turn into ashes" (from 'What Now, My Love') fell from those famously red Garland lips. Yet, despite her fatigued demeanour, nothing could compete with Judy's solo performance of 'Over The Rainbow', a song that, almost a century on, inhabits a place that so much popular music continues to strive for.

Years later, Liza Minnelli remarked that the Palladium shows signified the moment when "Mama realized that she had a grown-up daughter and that I wasn't a kid any more. [She] became very competitive with me. I wasn't Liza, but another woman in the same spotlight."

In January 1969, Judy Garland was once again on the Palladium stage, slurring her way through 'I Belong To London', and it was in London on 22 June that year that The Pride of the Palladium (she performed there a remarkable 68 times) was found dead, just days after her 47th birthday.

THE WHO
THE MARQUEE, LONDON, 24 NOVEMBER 1964–27 APRIL 1965

The Who underwent a remarkable transformation during their six-month residency at The Marquee. Only two weeks before co-managers Kit Lambert and Chris Stamp had hustled them a date on the quietest night of the week – Tuesday (24 November 1964) – they had been playing a residency at the Railway Hotel in Harrow and Wealdstone as The High Numbers. By the time the Marquee residency ended, on 27 April 1965, the band had a Top 10 hit single, were "faces" on television and magazine front pages, and had just started to record their debut album, *My Generation*.

More than that, The Who had become cheerleaders for a recent cultural phenomenon: the Mod. A dynamic assault on both eyes and ears, they epitomized everything the young Mod aspired to – stylish, speed-obsessed (in both senses of the word) and successful. As they continued to break box-office records at the Wardour Street club

that winter and spring, The Who aestheticized the pop world. Their music contained all the drama, flamboyance and aggression of everyday street life; their image was artful and iconic. And by the time The Who had quit their weekly spot at The Marquee, their feedback-drenched single, 'Anyway Anyhow Anywhere', was being promoted thus: "A pop-art group with a pop-art sound."

This didn't just happen by accident. "We realized that if the group were to build up any national following, we must take the West End," remembered Kit Lambert. A poor turnout on opening night was soon rectified by a relentless publicity campaign – fronted by the legendary "Maximum R&B" poster, black-and-white

Above: The Who, in action at The Marquee on 2 March 1967,
filmed for a German TV special.
Below right: Larking about before a Marquee show in 1965.

and acutely stylish. Some fans remember being given free whisky at
the club in a bid to enhance their appreciation of the band – not
that anyone really needed pepping up because The Who more than
lived up to their billing: they were extraordinary.

Guitarist Pete Townshend and bassist John Entwistle would
invariably turn their amps up to the max, Keith Moon virtually
redefined the role of a drummer with his theatrical, hyperactive
playing, while frontman Roger Daltrey often required a few drops of
the hard stuff himself if he wanted to be heard above the electric
storm. Even the sickening volume wasn't always enough for the
band. "We've got to the stage where we end the night by
destroying everything – which is expensive," Townshend told
reporters at the time. Happily, the management understood the
value of The Who's unquenchable desire for total commitment. "It's
an investment," shrugged Lambert – and one that soon paid off. By
the end of 1965, the Townshend-penned 'My Generation' neatly
summed up the truculent mood of the Marquee crowd and
universalized it.

PJ Proby

Fairfield Halls, Croydon, London, 29 January 1965

"I can't remember why we went to see PJ Proby at the Fairfield Halls. I don't know who else was on the bill and, unusually for me, I don't seem to have kept the ticket or any memento. He was quite a big name and I did quite like him, almost in a defiant way as he wasn't really cool, a sort of grubby version of Elvis. We weren't into Elvis at all, being definitely on the Mod rather than Rocker side of the spectrum, but we went and it was really exciting. What I remember most from that concert

in Croydon was that he put on a great, over the top, epic of a show.

"There was something really raunchy about PJ Proby. He was a real showman. He wore those terrific white shirts and boots, rather Heathcliffe-like, dark and brooding.

"At the Fairfield Halls the cheapest seats were in the choir stalls, which were at the back of the stage in a sort of semi-circle. We had seats at the front of the choir stalls but I can't remember sitting down at all. We spent a lot of time yelling for PJ to turn

round because we only had a back view. There was quite a big drop, about eight feet, from the choir stalls on to the back of the stage but we were hanging over it. Several girls had tried to climb onto the front of the stage, got quite close, and then got pulled back or thrown off.

"Suddenly climbing over the edge seemed the most obvious thing to do and I dropped down onto the stage. I ran across to PJ and planted a smacker on his cheek. He was hot and tanned and had a very

"He was hot and tanned, had a very smooth face, and smelled of sweat and make-up."

smooth face. I can actually remember what he smelt like – sweat and make-up! I was dragged off the side and out through a glass door into the corridor. I was rather terrified in case I was in the papers and my parents found out, but nothing happened.

"We had a phone number which I'm told we got from PJ's management in the foyer after the show. We crammed into a telephone box and phoned this number several times. Being sleuth-like, we realized we couldn't ask for PJ Proby, so we kept asking the man who answered if we could speak to Jim [his middle name] – very subtle! Eventually he got tired of hanging up and just stopped answering. It reminds me that we occasionally did mad things just because we could. I still have a soft spot in my memory for PJ. He went on to sing everything – rock'n'roll, Country and Western and he sang everything in someone else's style."

Jane, audience member

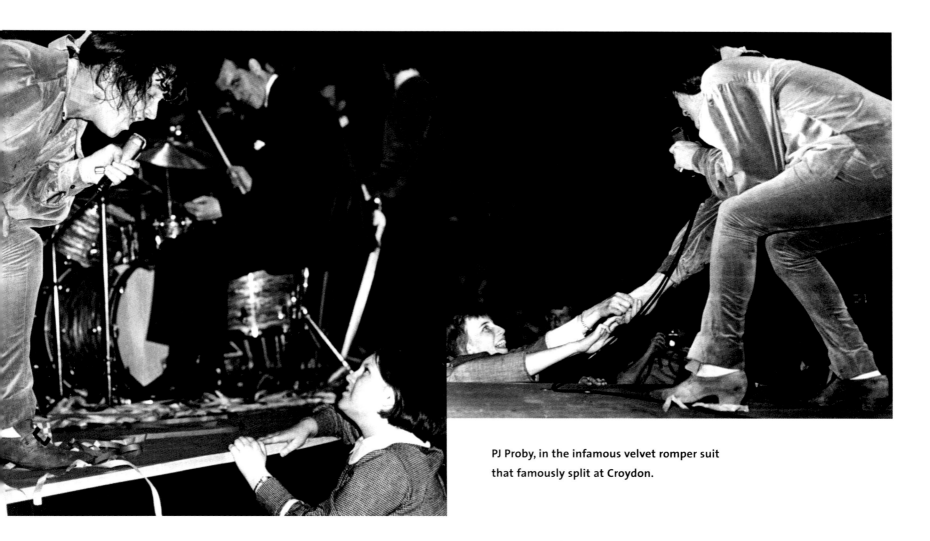

PJ Proby, in the infamous velvet romper suit that famously split at Croydon.

PJ Proby, Fairfield Halls, Croydon, 1965   59

THE TAMLA-MOTOWN REVUE

UK TOUR, MARCH–APRIL 1965

By spring 1965, the Motown label had notched up almost 30 Top 30 hits in the States and was officially known as "Hitsville, USA". It was a different story in Britain where, despite recent inroads made by The Supremes and Martha And The Vandellas, "the sound of young America" had yet to make a significant dent in the parochial British charts. That was all too evident when The Tamla-Motown Revue rolled in on 19 March 1965 for a whistle-stop tour of 21 shows in 24 days as part of a wider European visit, for despite its cast of superstars-in-the-making – The Miracles, The Supremes, "Little" Stevie Wonder, Martha And The Vandellas and the Motown backing band led by Earl Van Dyke – the Revue managed to create all the wrong kind of headlines.

"THE INVASION GOES WRONG", declared the *Daily Express*, citing poor ticket sales, particularly in the provinces. Even the last-minute addition of the homegrown 'Yeh Yeh' chart-topper Georgie Fame failed to prevent nights such as the one in Kingston-upon-Thames, where the promoter was reduced to giving away a thousand tickets in a bid to spare the performers' blushes. It was reported that fewer than 200 turned up at the ABC in Chester. "There were more people on stage than in the audience," admitted Dave Godin, Motown's British consultant, recalling another no-show in Cardiff. Suggestions that label boss Berry Gordy Jr was Detroit's answer to Brian Epstein suddenly seemed hopelessly premature. To make matters worse, the stars complained about the British food, the backing band threatened to strike over pay, and at one point Martha Reeves was packed off to Scotland to cool down after a run-in with Gordy.

It had been a different story on opening night in London, where Dusty Springfield joined a packed and wildly enthusiastic crowd at the Finsbury Park Astoria. For those hip to the brand-new beat, The Tamla-Motown Revue was a slickly choreographed, hit-packed show and a unique opportunity to see many of the artists talked up in the British press by The Beatles and The Stones, but it was for aficionados only. Although 'My Guy' singer Mary Wells had toured with The Beatles, and Kim Weston did the rounds with Gerry And The Pacemakers later in '64, the label's profile in Britain still largely rested on hearsay. The Supremes' 'Where Did Our Love Go' and the chart-topping 'Baby Love' had begun to turn things around, but a good indication of the label's cult status came in autumn '64 when Martha And The Vandellas' irresistible anthem 'Dancing In The Street' stalled at number 28 in Britain.

The Tamla-Motown Revue had been cooked up to coincide with a new record label launch, and was intended to stamp the company's name and sound all over Britain, but it was premature. Not, though, for those quick enough to catch Martha And The Vandellas bringing the first half to fever pitch with 'Heatwave', 'Nowhere To Run' and 'Dancing In The Street', harmonica-wielding "Little" Stevie Wonder delighting with 'Fingertips', The Supremes raising their arms in unison for their latest hit, 'Stop! In The Name Of Love', before closing with Sam Cooke's 'Shake', and The Miracles slowing the tempo right down for 'Ooh Baby Baby' before closing the show with an invigorating 'Mickey's Monkey'. By the time a second package tour rolled into Britain in September 1966, everything had changed. Tamla-Motown and its fabulous roster of artists had become household names.

Previous page, left: The Supremes, fast becoming Motown's biggest export.

Previous page right: Motown superstars in the making, including "Little" Stevie Wonder (centre).

Above: Martha Reeves (right) with her Mandellas.

Right: Smokey Robinson And The Miracles always closed the shows with a breathtaking 'Mickey's Monkey'.

Opposite: How sweet it is to be in England. But awaiting Marvin Gaye and his stable-mates were half empty venues and negative publicity.

The Tamla-Motown Revue, UK, 1965

INTERNATIONAL POETRY READING

ROYAL ALBERT HALL, LONDON, 11 JUNE 1965

Opposite: Visiting beat poet Allen Ginsberg. Days earlier, he'd "gone naked" at his birthday party. "You don't do that in front of the birds," advised John Lennon.

Bottom left: Michael Horowitz, a crucial figure in the fast-emerging alternative scene.

Right: Ginsberg and gang on the steps of the Albert Memorial. Barbara Rubin (with camera), (back row) Adrian Mitchell, Anselm Hollo, Marcus Field, Mike Horovitz, Ernst Jandl, (front row) Harry Fainlight, Alex Trocchi, Allen Ginsberg, John Esam, Dan Richter.

"The Albert Hall poetry event marked the beginning of the tsunami of 1967, though only as it receded in time could you see its significance. The whole thing was set up in just a few days. It wasn't really planned. It was more a psychic blast, and at the centre of that was Barbara Rubin, who was trying to be Ginsberg's girlfriend at the time. While the impetus came from a bunch of visiting Americans, the scene was ripe for it. We had no idea it would be such a success. It was nicely full. You looked around, saw 6,000–7,000 people and thought, Christ, there's that many of us!

"The counterculture would be one way of describing it, or the underground, though that hadn't quite blossomed by that point. There was clearly some kind of cultural pressure building up. Mike Horowitz, one of the leading English poets, had been combining jazz and poetry for about six or seven years before that. He turned a lot of people on to that sort of alternative culture.

"The event brought together artists from various fields, from Julie Felix, who was a young folksinger, to Felix Topolski, who was an ageing graphic artist. Mainly, it was about the poets. Ginsberg didn't seem to have a very good time, but all the leading British poets such as Christopher Logue and Adrian Mitchell were there. Writers turned up from as far away as Austria and Russia.

"The atmosphere was less one of reverence than of absorption in the moment. Before the Albert Hall was 'The Happening'. A Happening was an event where a bunch of people get together and you don't quite know what's going to happen. The Fluxus group in the early 60s specialized in Happenings. You might be enveloped in smoke from a machine while trying to watch a movie over which people were playing flutes. There was a genuine element of spontaneity. And although most people were sitting down in the Albert Hall, the Happening concept seemed to inform the event. There were other influences – CND [Campaign for nuclear disarmament], for example, and politics. In 1964, Harold Wilson won the election for Labour. And after the election, he immediately turned round from being anti-nuclear to pronuclear. That pissed a lot of people off. I was so pissed off I didn't vote for the next 30 years! And then there was dope, which was also becoming popular. My nose doesn't remember the smell of that in the hall, but there was definitely incense there. There was all this cross-cultural stuff going on. And in the mid-60s, that was just part of the general attitude, being open to all these things. It wasn't just about music."

John 'Hoppy' Hopkins, press officer

66   **International Poetry Reading, Royal Albert Hall, London, 1965**

Beatlemania didn't come any bigger than this, with 55,000 fans screaming, waving banners and struggling to gain a glimpse of The Fab Four through walls of security wire. Hundreds of yards away, on a makeshift stage in the middle of a huge baseball stadium, four musicians attempted to make themselves heard through specially commissioned 100-watt Vox amps and a PA system better suited to a voice reading out baseball scores. "It was the biggest live show anybody's ever done," enthused John Lennon some time later, "and it was fantastic, the most exciting."

Moments before running out on to the field in their matching military-style beige jackets, The Beatles resembled a bunch of reluctant heroes, weary at the prospect of yet another American tour. They had only just completed a jaunt around Europe, and Shea Stadium marked the start of a further dozen or so huge American shows. Even getting there had been exhausting. From Wall Street, they had taken a helicopter flight, ending up on a roof at the World's Fair, where an armoured vehicle was waiting to ferry them to the stadium.

Once they were into their 12-song set, much of it barely audible over the ear-piercing din of the audience, The Beatles' old professionalism saw them through. John Lennon even delivered an impressive impersonation of Jerry Lee Lewis at the keyboard during a blistering 'I'm Down', though both he and his colleagues knew that his increasingly erratic behaviour was no longer merely an act. "I'd cracked up," he admitted many years later.

The Beatles, Shea Stadium, New York, 1965

From Trips
To Tragedy

REACHING A BEATLES-INDUCED, JUMP-CUT AND STYLISHLY MONOCHROME PEAK IN 1964 AND 65, THE WORLD SUDDENLY TURNED DAY-GLO SOME TIME IN 1966. DRUGS, ESPECIALLY LSD, THAT ONCE-TRIED, NEVER FORGOTTEN TRIP TO ANOTHER DIMENSION, HAD SOMETHING TO DO WITH IT. SO, TOO, DID TECHNOLOGY, WHICH HAD GROWN SO ADVANCED THAT BOTH SOUND AND VISUALS WERE INCREASINGLY ABLE TO MIRROR THE WILDER EXCESSES OF THE ACID TRIP. "NOTHING IS REAL," SANG A BLISSED OUT JOHN LENNON ON 'STRAWBERRY FIELDS FOREVER', THE SONG THAT REMAINS UNSURPASSED AS THE MOST PERFECT THREE-MINUTE MUSICAL DEFINITION OF PSYCHEDELIA. (THOUGH THE BEACH BOYS' 'GOOD VIBRATIONS' IS ONLY A MICRO-MOMENT BEHIND.) AND, OUTSIDE INTERMITTENT PERIODS OF WAR, RARELY HAD SUCH A COLLECTIVE FLIGHT FROM REALITY GRIPPED AN ENTIRE GENERATION.

DURING THESE REMARKABLE YEARS, YOUTH CULTURE WAS MAKING ALL THE ADVANCES. THE SCREAMS OF THE BEAT ERA HAD MELTED INTO (PSEUDO-)PHILOSOPHICAL INTROSPECTION; POCKET-MONEY NOW MATTERED LESS THAN POLITICS; WHILE CONCERT-GOING WAS NO LONGER A RITUAL WHOLLY CONTROLLED BY THE OLD-FASHIONED ENTERTAINMENT BUSINESS. THAT "STRANGE VIBRATION" SCOTT MCKENZIE HAD SUNG ABOUT ON 'SAN FRANCISCO (BE SURE TO WEAR FLOWERS IN YOUR HAIR)' BEGAN TO HIT EVERY TOWN AND CITY IN THE WESTERN WORLD, WHERE AN ALTERNATIVE CULTURE WAS FAST EMERGING TO CHALLENGE THE VALUES OF 'STRAIGHT SOCIETY'.

ROCK CONCERTS PROVIDED A CRUCIAL MEETING-PLACE FOR THE COUNTERCULTURE, THOUGH GIG-GOING WAS NOW AN ACT OF LIFESTYLE ALLEGIANCE AS MUCH AS AN ENTERTAINMENT RITUAL. CLUBS SPRANG UP IN HITHERTO UNUTILIZED SPACES, SUCH AS ALL SAINTS HALL WHERE THE PINK FLOYD FLOURISHED. AND POP FESTIVALS PROLIFERATED, AS IF TO PRESAGE THE ARRIVAL OF A NEW AQUARIAN AGE OF COMMUNALITY AND HARMONY. BUT NOT EVERYTHING HAD CHANGED. FRANK SINATRA STILL PERFORMED IN TRADITIONAL WATERING-HOLES WHERE OLD-STYLE GLITZ AND GLAMOUR REMAINED RESOLUTELY ON THE MENU. BUT EVEN HE'D BEGUN TO SLIP A CRAVAT AROUND HIS NECK. HE'D ALSO FOUND HIMSELF A HIP NEW DATE IN MIA FARROW, THE ELFIN HOLLYWOOD HIPPIE-CHICK WHO SUBSEQUENTLY DITCHED FRANK FOR MYSTICISM WHEN SHE JOINED THE BEATLES AT THE MAHARISHI'S HIMALAYAN HIDEAWAY IN SPRING 1968. TWO YEARS LATER, THE FAB FOUR WERE NO MORE, AND ALL THOSE HIPPIE HOPES HAD TURNED SOUR, A SITUATION HASTENED BY THE MANSON MURDERS AND THE TRAGEDY THAT TOOK PLACE UNDER THE NOSES OF THE ROLLING STONES AT ALTAMONT. FROM LOVE TO HATE IN ONE CHAPTER...

Trips Festival

Longshoreman's Hall, San Francisco, 21–23 January 1966

"Can YOU pass the acid test?" was the question posed at this landmark weekend in the history of psychedelia. Many already had – Ken Kesey and his Merry Pranksters had been holding LSD-fuelled "acid test" parties in San Francisco for months – but never on a scale such as this.

Around 10,000 attended this three-day event, many coming in for free, thanks to Ken Kesey holding open the back door, rather than paying the $2 entrance fee ($5 for the entire weekend). With at least five film screens, various light and slide shows, stalls selling alternative books and paraphernalia and several rock'n'roll bands – including The Grateful Dead and Big Brother And The Holding Company – the Trips Festival was an organizational triumph that established the notion of a vibrant, fast-growing alternative culture. Bill Graham, soon to become the Bay Area's most famous entrepreneur, helmed the event.

The Bay Area's influential, larger-than-life commentator Ralph J Gleason enthused about the event in the *San Francisco Chronicle* under the misleading heading "ONE WILD NIGHT – A TRIPS FESTIVAL". "The variety, imagination, degrees of exoticism and just plain freaky far-outness of the thousands who thronged the Longshore [*sic*] Hall defies description," he claimed. Gleason admitted, however, that the omens were not good on opening night.

According to the Wes Wilson-designed flyer, Friday night promised "slides, movies, sound tracks, flowers, food, rock'n'roll, eagle lone whistle, Indians..." It was, reckoned Gleason, a bore. Worse still, one trippy hippie told him: "This is a bore even on acid." Some *avant-garde* theatre, supplemented with a few projections of Indians on a screen, was clearly inadequate to enhance the high.

Everything came alive on Saturday night. The audience, some in Indian headgear, others in hooped Breton shirts, others still bare-chested and dancing ecstatically, their eyes closed in blissful abandon, weaved in and out of the technicolour shadows. Hell's Angels grinned. Allen Ginsberg wandered guru-like. One man, head-to-toe in bandages and with only his eyes visible, wore a sign around his neck that read: "You're in the Pepsi generation and I'm a pimply freak." The Grateful Dead and Big Brother provided the "psychedelic symphony" promised on the posters.

By the third and final night, the cops had been dosed and were now more interested in playing with model aircraft than in policing the event. Even disapproving Lenny Lipton from the *Berkeley Barb* managed to make it all sound positively appealing: "Topless chick and man with hands over tits with 4,000 gaping fruits...You know what it looked like? For all the world like the Stardust ballroom."

"The TRIP – or electronic performance – is a new medium of communication and entertainment."
Extract from Trips Festival flyer

"The general tone of things has moved on from the self-conscious happening to a more JUBILANT occasion where the audience PARTICIPATES because it's more fun to do so that not...Maybe this is the ROCK REVOLUTION. Audience dancing is an assumed part of all the shows, and the audience is invited to wear ECSTATIC DRESS and bring their own GADGETS..."

ADVANCE PUBLICITY FOR THE TRIPS FESTIVAL

VELVET UNDERGROUND
THE DOM, ST MARK'S PLACE, NEW YORK, APRIL 1966

"Andy Warhol was invited to put together a happening, an environmental event, so he projected movies on the walls, put a light show together, he had the Velvet Underground play and asked for some kind of theatre. Gerard [Malanga] provided that. He came up with the flashing strobe lights, he dressed me and gave me a whip. Before this, rock'n'roll bands literally just played for an audience.

"Gerard and I danced in front of the Velvets while films played behind us. The dances were structured. For 'Heroin', we had these large plastic needles. I lifted weights during 'I'm Waiting For The Man'. There was a heavy S&M motif, too, which I was entirely familiar with because of my

work with the Theatre of the Ridiculous. It was less about dancing than performance. We didn't just 'do the Watusi'. It was very improvised, so things got weirder and weirder. Sometimes Ingrid [Superstar] or Ronnie [Cutrone] would join us.

"The Dom was a large Polish dance hall with a stage, a balcony and a large floor. There was no bar, and except for the mirror ball and the flickering lights on stage, it was almost entirely black. The place was always crowded. Warhol would stand in the balcony and watch everything. Sometimes we'd dance with the crowd, though it wasn't really dancing. It was a more organic thing, very expressionistic. The audience were strangers, mostly young, and I think they were into drugs...

"There was nothing psychedelic about it. Except maybe the light show. Nobody liked acid. Acid was used on the West Coast. We used amphetamine. On the West Coast, they dressed in colours. We dressed in black and white. It was anti-psychedelic. On the West Coast, you could see the back of someone's mind, like 'Wow!' But we had these tremendous discussions about Heidegger and stuff. It was very different. There was free love on the West Coast, and nudity. We didn't like nudity. We didn't like bare feet. We always wore boots. We were not into free love. We were very S&M. Uptight? Yeah, maybe the Dom shows went under that title. I can't remember. We might have been transforming reality, but it was definitely not psychedelic. I can't use that word."

Mary Woronov, dancer

Opposite: The Grateful Dead's Bob Weir and Phil Lesh, dark stars of the emerging San Francisco psychedelic underground.

"The band always stood still. They didn't even look at the audience. It was as if the audience wasn't there."
MARY WORONOV

Velvet Underground, The Dom, New York, 1966

"Bob put his feelings over to the knockers just great. When someone shouted out to him 'Judas!', he just calmly went to the microphone and quietly drawled, 'Ya liar.' "

OLDHAM EVENING CHRONICLE,
25 MAY 1966

Bob Dylan And The Hawks

"Judas!"

The most famous heckle in popular music was uttered by Keith Butler, a 20-year-old student incensed by Dylan's loud embrace of amplified rock'n'roll music. While Butler took 30 years to declare himself the perpetrator, Dylan took only a few moments before spitting out his reply: "I don't believe you! You're a liar!" he snarled, before adding an indignant "Play fuckin' loud!" to his backing band. That was the cue for a knife-edge finale of 'Like A Rolling Stone', the song that had first announced a new electrified Dylan to the wider world the previous summer.

'Like A Rolling Stone' accelerated the "betrayal" debate that had been prompted by Dylan's fast-accelerating departure from the protest songs of his early career. By 1965, his verse owed as much to surrealism as it did to Woody Guthrie, and the simple finger-picked guitar accompaniment he had become famous for had now been augmented by a swelling rock-band sound. Even Dylan's earnest hobo image had been dropped in favour of a shock-headed, tight-suited, shades-sporting bohemian look. In interviews, Dylan's most pressing commitment no longer seemed to be to the Little Man or the Big Idea, but to himself.

By the time Dylan's rock circus rolled into Manchester, he and his electric band – later known simply as The Band – had been performing together since the previous August...and they rocked. A majority of the crowd simply accepted the change, but at the outer fringes a battle still raged. The rucksack-carrying folkies still hung on to Dylan as the voice of the (increasingly nebulous) protest movement. Others regarded him as the hip priest of pop, who was fast elevating popular music to a thrilling new art form.

The Beatles, The Rolling Stones, folk-rock newcomers The Byrds and everyone else who aspired to pop greatness had been deeply affected by Dylan's recent transformation – and intimidated. Dylan had become a law unto himself. However, even this iconoclast understood the value in not completely alienating his original audience. Like all the UK shows, the Manchester gig was neatly divided into two sections, an acoustic set that largely comprised recent and new material, followed by an eight-song electric performance, that included drastically reworked versions of material from some of his troubadour albums.

The first set was greeted with a hushed reverence that was typical of Dylan's earlier shows. The lyricism of songs such as 'Visions Of Johanna' and 'Desolation Row' were a far cry from earlier, plain-speaking anthems such as 'Blowin' In The Wind' (notably absent from the 1966 set lists), but this was Dylan unadorned and that was what mattered. Those who regarded the group format as tawdry and somehow inauthentic were suitably swayed.

The mood changed after the intermission. Dylan re-emerged with a Fender Stratocaster round his neck and with the battle scars of previous shows, which had witnessed numerous walkouts and catcalls, all too visible in his belligerent manner and body language. By the end of the second song, 'I Don't Believe You', which had been transformed from a piquant acoustic ballad into a robust rock put-down, a section of the Manchester crowd had begun to slow handclap. Dylan responded by blowing a few trad-style notes on his harmonica, before launching into a dramatically reworked version of one of his earliest recordings, 'Baby, Let Me Follow You Down'. Towards the end of the set, he mumbled an incomprehensible tale into the mic, affronting the audience with wilful obscurity. Then along came the spectre of Judas, and a notable gig thus became a legendary one.

Acoustic set

'She Belongs to Me'
'Fourth Time Around'
'Visions Of Johanna'
'It's All Over Now, Baby Blue'
'Desolation Row'
'Just Like A Woman'
'Mr Tambourine Man'

Electric set

'Tell Me, Momma'
'I Don't Believe You'
'Baby, Let Me Follow You Down'
'Just Like Tom Thumb's Blues'
'Leopard-Skin Pill-Box Hat'
'One Too Many Mornings'
'Ballad Of A Thin Man'
'Like A Rolling Stone'

Bob Dylan And The Hawks, Free Trade Hall, Manchester, 1966

Overleaf, top: Legendary bandleader Count Basie accompanied Sinatra for his January 1966 season at The Sands.

Right: Dean Martin (left), Sammy Davis Jr (second from left) and Frank Sinatra (third from right). Those guys stood at the centre of the world," believed Sinatra's daughter, Nancy.

Bob Dylan And The Hawks, Free Trade Hall, Manchester, 1966 81

FRANK SINATRA
THE SANDS, LAS VEGAS, 1966

Frank Sinatra didn't like rock'n'roll. "(It) smells phony and false...the most brutal, ugly, desperate, vicious form of expression it has been my misfortune to hear," he complained in 1957. Back in favour after his Academy Award-winning role in *From Here To Eternity*, Sinatra preferred his entertainment the traditional way: a mix of standards and comedy routines, performed in formal wear, and accompanied by the clink of champagne glasses and the sound of a rapidly spinning roulette wheel – and there was no better place for that than The Sands, Las Vegas's self-styled "Place In The Sun" and a mainstay of Sinatra's social whirl since it opened in 1952.

Widely rumoured to have been funded by mob money, The Sands boasted an impressive clientele, from future President John F Kennedy to film stars and shadier figures carrying suitcases full of notes and Colt 45s in their belts. By the early '60s, Sinatra had become a key figure in the Sands Corporation and a regular performer in the hotel's Copa Room. Nancy Sinatra saw her father perform there alongside Dean Martin and Sammy Davis Jr in September 1963. "The centre of the world was where these guys were standing," she proudly recalled.

Sinatra's Sands swansong came three years later, just as he'd made his peace with the rock'n'roll generation thanks to the success of the chart-topping 'Strangers In The Night'. He was there in January 1966 with the Count Basie Orchestra, conducted by Quincy Jones. Back for three weeks in April, he returned again for a final two-week residency in November, accompanied by the 34-piece Antonio Morelli Orchestra. "Sinatra looks and sounds better than ever," raved *Variety*. "He's obviously having a very good year." The following year wasn't bad either, with 'Something Stupid', his strangely affectionate duet with daughter Nancy, giving him another Number 1 hit. However, when Howard Hughes steamed in with a successful, multi-million dollar bid for his favourite Vegas haunt, Sinatra's Sands days came to an end.

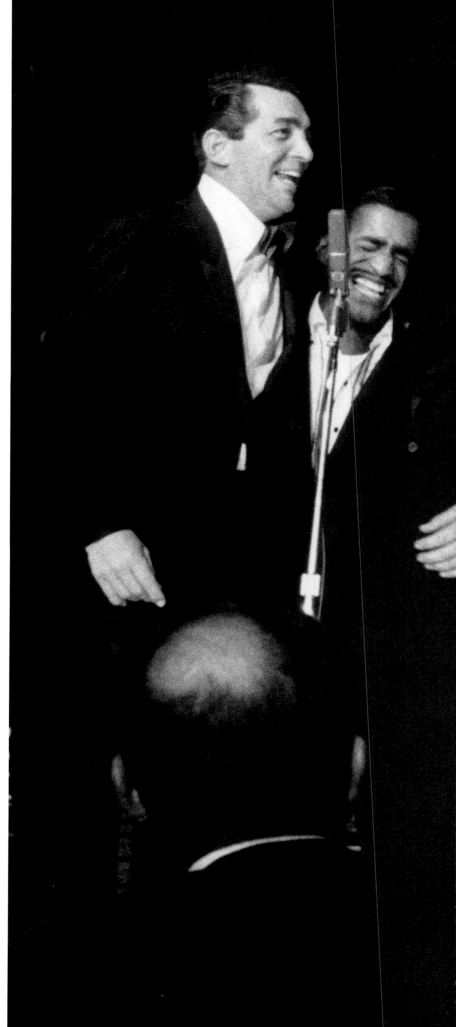

THE PINK FLOYD
ALL SAINTS CHURCH HALL, POWIS GARDENS, NOTTING HILL, LONDON, 1966

"The Powis Gardens gigs marked the beginning of our popularity," says Pink Floyd conceptualist/bassist Roger Waters. "It was an exciting time. Syd [Barrett] was still functioning, and we were all very enthusiastic. It was way before we turned pro and started making records." And, in the vernacular of the time, it was "way out".

The British psychedelic freak-out may have been imported from the American West Coast, but as this inaugural series of gigs held in a nondescript church hall in Notting Hill confirmed, it was by no means its mirror image.

"Our lights were much less blippy and more image-filled, despite the fact that we had an American do them at the All Saints Hall gigs," says The Pink Floyd's original co-manager Peter Jenner. "Our shows were more dark and druggy, with all these powerful, expressionistic shadows. Very Nosferatu."

By autumn 1966, psychedelia was being featured in the national media, which initially regarded it as simply the latest trend to replace beat, mod and miniskirts. "We didn't really know what psychedelia was," says Floyd drummer Nick Mason. "There was the drug experience, but it was a pretty muddled philosophy, made up of a whole bunch of fashionable ideas. In essence, it was about pushing boundaries..."

Billing themselves as a "sound/light wordshop", and name checking acid guru Dr Timothy Leary's mantra "Turn on, tune in, drop out" on their concert posters, The Pink Floyd epitomized the era's "anything goes" philosophy. Reviewing one of the Powis Gardens performances, underground journal *International Times* declared approvingly that "their work is largely improvisational".

"We needed to project what we were doing as more important than pop songs, that it was culture, revolutionary culture," says Jenner. And it worked. During the group's short residency as fundraisers for John "Hoppy" Hopkins' community education project known as the London Free School, The Floyd were interviewed for *The Times* and attracted a rag-bag of students, intellectuals and bohemians to their Notting Hill shows. Many came with the express intention of enhancing their acid trip with a suitably mind-boggling light and sound experience.

"It wasn't a conscious decision to play trip music," insists Nick Mason. "It was simply us reacting to a visual stimulus, which was particularly ill-suited to choruses and middle eights." And thus a peculiarly English strand of psychedelic music was born.

The Pink Floyd, All Saints Church Hall, London, 1966   85

"It was at All Saints Hall that we started showing bubbly slides on the walls. We got people to put coloured inks between pieces of glass and heat them up. And jolly nice it looked, too." ROGER WATERS

THE STAX/VOLT TOUR
BRITAIN AND PARIS, 17 MARCH–2 APRIL 1967

It would be, claimed the tour poster with some justification, "The Greatest Ever 'Soul' Show". Yes, Otis Redding was back in town, this time accompanied by virtually the entire Stax Records hit factory from Memphis, Tennessee, including half a dozen of the hottest soul singers, plus the ultimate tight-but-loose backing of Booker T. And The MGs. The result was a masterclass in package tour dynamics of a kind that was rarely witnessed again. Even the musicians were taken aback as their performances grew stronger, and the scenes ever more hysterical, with each successive show.

"We were expecting to sneak into the country," MGs guitarist Steve Cropper told soul music chronicler Gerri Hirshey, but with soul sounds starting to dominate on the dance floor, and many of the visiting stars already recognized names among in-crowders, the Stax/Volt artists were feted everywhere they went during their 12-date "Hit the Road Stax" jaunt. "It was just a mind-

blower," Cropper told Peter Guralnick. "[It] was something that happened to Elvis or Ricky Nelson, but it didn't happen to the Stax/Volt band. It didn't happen to Booker T And The MGs."

But it did. From the moment Booker T And The MGs kicked off the show with a groovy, fast-paced instrumental, the crowd was on its feet and eager to be taken higher. After a short set from horn section The Mar-Keys, Otis Redding protégé Arthur Conley, the only non-Stax artist on the bill, stepped forward, thrilling the crowds with his new single, 'Sweet Soul Music'. Carla Thomas, who due to a prior commitment back in the States was replaced by

Otis Redding performs on *Ready, Steady, Go!*, wearing his famously just-too-tight trousers.

Overleaf: Carla Thomas and the legendary Booker T And The MGs.

Stax/Volt Tour, Britain and Paris, 1967

Sharon Tandy midway through the tour, brought the first half of the show to a close with a set that included rapturously received versions of her US hits 'B-A-B-Y' and 'Something Good'. "Outta sight!" was the verdict of MC Emperor Rosko at the Finsbury Park Astoria on the tour's opening night in London.

After a second set from the MGs, Eddie Floyd's stint at the mic included his recent US hit 'Knock On Wood', before Sam And Dave took the night by the scruff of its neck with an astonishing display of fleet-footedness and dynamic, double-barrel vocalizing. These 'Hold On I'm A Comin'' stars were a tough act for anyone to follow, and Otis Redding's manager Phil Walden knew it. "They may well have been the best live act ever," he admitted years later, "so Otis had to work for his money."

But then the incendiary Otis Redding, the farmer's son from Macon, Georgia, who saw himself as the Love Crowd's Sam Cooke, always worked hard for his money. A musical all-rounder who one minute would shamelessly flatter the crowd ("It's good to be back home!" he told the Finsbury Park audience), and the next be discharging the deepest soul you'd ever heard, Otis was the entertainer of the moment. He'd sing The Beatles' 'Day Tripper', Smokey Robinson's 'My Girl' and Sam Cooke's 'Shake' as if they were his own. He'd sing his own anthem, 'Respect', and make it belong to everyone. Better still, the man in the just-too-tight trousers would work a song like 'I've Been Loving You Too Long', or his pièce de résistance 'Try A Little Tenderness', into a climax that shattered the pain/pleasure threshold to become almost unbearable.

Professional and sophisticated, yet heartstoppingly true, Otis Redding had it all – which made it all the more tragic when he was killed in a plane crash just nine months after everything suggested that pop superstardom was his for the taking.

THE 14-HOUR TECHNICOLOR DREAM

ALEXANDRA PALACE, LONDON, 29 APRIL 1967

"I remember standing in the middle of the place in the afternoon and thinking, 'How does this space get filled? Are there enough freaks?' But there were, and a lot of freakily dressed people too. When *IT* magazine started in October 1966, the underground had only existed in this network of people's flats. Then the UFO Club opened, and by the spring the streets of London were showing the first visible signs that something big was going on.

"The idea for the 'Dream' was hatched in Jack Moore's flat in Covent Garden, just after *IT* had been busted by the Obscene Publications Squad in March. I was asked to design the poster. As we talked, I remember focusing on an ashtray, attempting to make a metaphor involving ashtrays and the state we were in. That's indicative of my memory of the event, too. There was this pre-drug state and post-drug, post-party state, but between times...?

"I was all over the place – trying to help while at the same time getting out of my head, chatting, spinning, idiot dancing. I don't remember much about the bands at all. The groups were set up at either end, but Ally Pally is a big place, so it was easy to lose the sound and fade off into something else. There were lots of parties within parties, stalls selling tie-dye shirts, a huge fairground helter skelter, film shows, improvised dance performances. Above all, once the darkness of the evening brought the event to life, the drugs took over.

"I loved this idea of taking over a space so that it becomes something else for a night,

alexis korner
alex harvey
creation
charlie brown's
clowns
champion jack
dupree
denny laine
gary farr
graham bond
ginger johnson
jacobs ladder
construction co.
move
one one seven
pink floyd
poetry band
purple gang
pretty things
pete townshend
poison bellows
soft machine
sun trolley
socibl deviants
stalkers
the utterly incredibl
too long ago
to remember
sometimes shouting
at people
marc sullivan
martin doughty
maureen pape
john pape
mike stocks
noel murphy
dave russell
christopher logue
barry fantoni
ron geeson
john fahey
mike horowitz
alex trocchi
mike kenshall
yoko ono
binder edwards
& vaughan
26 kingly street
the flies
robert randell

international times
free speech benefit
alexandra palace N.22
8pm saturday
29 april»sun30
tickets £1
in advance»only
indica better books colletts
dobells dave curtis 57 greek
st w.1 ger 1548 and main
it distributors
oryour local agent
bus shuttle from wood green⊖
highgate⊖ 8:12pm

14
HOUR
Technicolor Dream

and Ally Pally was an amazing place for such an event – and appropriate too, being a palace. It was a Utopian feeling. There's no question it felt very genuine. You were sharing things with other people. It was no longer about being an audience that had come to see the star on stage. It was simply the idea of being there, being with a tribe of like-minded people. No longer 'I Was There' but 'We Were There'. Later on, it all got so much bigger, with events like Woodstock and Hyde Park.

"It was an all-nighter, and I have very clear recollections of people wandering around outside the next morning, blinking into the dawn, and turning around to look at the place you had just spent a huge amount of time off your head in. Very special!"

Mike McInnerney, poster designer

Above right: The Sam Gopal Band, one of dozens who played through the night on two different stages.

Right: Beatle John Lennon drifts through the crowds.

Far right: A couple await the event dressed in the season's fineries.

Opposite: Weird scenes inside the palace.

The 14-Hour Technicolor Dream, London, 1967 91

THE MONTEREY INTERNATIONAL POP FESTIVAL

MONTEREY, CALIFORNIA, 16–18 JUNE 1967

The publicity gently promised a weekend of "music, love and flowers". The 175,000 pleasure seekers who made it to Monterey, some 100 miles south of psychedelic central San Francisco, experienced all that and more, for Monterey was that genuine summer-of-love moment. With Scott McKenzie's 'San Francisco (Be Sure To Wear Flowers In Your Hair)' poised to top charts around the world, flower power no longer seemed like a fantasy for the few, but an attainable reality for the entire western world. Youth spoke with one voice, and the message was...love.

In truth, Monterey marked an uneasy alliance between the commune-dwelling hipsters from San Francisco's Haight-Ashbury district and the more traditionally minded moneyed hustlers from Los Angeles. Musically, too, its palette was pleasingly broad: The Who's violent electric rock, spiritual serenity from Indian sitar player Ravi Shankar, the deep soul of Otis Redding and the psychedelic sounds of the emerging West Coast high flyers. For three days, this new-fangled musical eclecticism worked.

Organized by an international committee that included various members of The Beatles, The Rolling Stones, The Byrds, The Beach Boys and The Mamas And The Papas, Monterey defined the idea of a music festival for years to come. It caught the youth revolution in transition, as pop's innocence was fast being eclipsed by a new, more purposeful rock culture. Anti-war and anti-establishment, pro-drugs and free love, the hippie subculture had a whole new bunch of messengers – most of whom found international fame at Monterey.

Jimi Hendrix sacrificed his guitar. The Who smashed up their equipment. Otis Redding wowed what he called "the love crowd". Ravi Shankar reduced them to blissful silence. Janis Joplin went down so well that she was asked to perform the next day. A bad batch of "Monterey purple" sent some running to "the bummer tent". Half a million dollars was raised for charity. Later, there was a full-length feature film, *Monterey Pop*, and a four-CD box set, but according to Dennis Hopper, you really had to be there. "The vibe was beautiful," he said. It was "the purest, most beautiful moment of the whole '60s trip".

The Performers

Friday

The Association
The Paupers
Lou Rawls
Beverly
Johnny Rivers
Eric Burdon And The Animals
Simon And Garfunkel

Saturday

Canned Heat
Big Brother And The Holding Company
    featuring Janis Joplin
Country Joe And The Fish
Al Kooper
The Butterfield Blues Band
Quicksilver Messenger Service
The Steve Miller Band
The Electric Flag
Moby Grape
Hugh Masekela
The Byrds
Laura Nyro
Jefferson Airplane
Booker T And The MGs with the Mar-Keys
Otis Redding

Sunday

Ravi Shankar
The Blues Project
Big Brother And The Holding Company
    featuring Janis Joplin
The Group With No Name
Buffalo Springfield
The Who
The Grateful Dead
The Jimi Hendrix Experience
Scott McKenzie
The Mamas And The Papas

Previous page, top left: The Mamas And The Papas' John Phillips, a prime mover in getting the festival underway.

Middle: Hippie Animal, Eric Burdon.

Bottom: The Monterey audience arrived in various shades of day-glo.

Right: Jimi Hendrix lights up.

This page, opposite: The Byrds, whose David Crosby (right) dedicated one song, 'He Was A Friend Of Mine', to the late President Kennedy.

Top left: Original Velvet Underground chanteuse Nico, with Rolling Stone Brian Jones. The Stones' guitarist had flown over from London to introduce Jimi Hendrix to an unsuspecting American audience.

Bottom left: Big Brother And The Holding Company, fronted by a glittering Janis Joplin, went down so well that the organizers asked them back to play a second set.

Monterey Pop Festival, 1967   95

JOHNNY CASH

It was not the first time Johnny Cash had seen the inside of a prison. He had been locked up several times over the years, usually for some minor public order or drugs offence, and ever since New Year's Day in 1958, when he performed in a rain-swept yard in San Quentin, watched by inmate and fellow country legend Merle Haggard, Cash had intermittently performed for the boys wearing the wrong shade of blue.

By 1967, Johnny Cash was down on his luck again. The best years of his career seemed way behind him, but with the support of a new producer, Bob Johnston, and a green light from Governor Ronald Reagan, in January, 1968 he gave the performance of a lifetime in front of 1,000 inmates at Folsom State Prison in California. "There was something in him that drew him to these men," remembered his wife, June Carter Cash.

Dressed in his customary black, and perched on a white stool with a small combo behind him, the amphetamine-driven Cash introduced himself with the immortal words "Hello, I'm Johnny Cash…" before launching right into 'Folsom Prison Blues'. The performance was a triumph, the resulting live record his best-selling yet, and shortly afterwards when he married June Carter, who was determined to clean him up, the man in black was back on track.

Little over a year later, on 24 February 1969, Cash repeated his prison exercise, this time down in San Quentin State Prison, overlooking San Francisco Bay, with a larger ensemble and a wider-ranging repertoire (including his novelty hit 'A Boy Named Sue'). It was, June recalled, the day they had "come to see the lost and lonely ones". As Cash sauntered on stage, she remembered the depth of feeling in the room, even if she struggled to explain it. "I don't know if explode is the word or not," she wrote, but "some kind of internal energy for those men – the prisoners, the guards, even the warden – gave way to anger, to love and to laughter…a reaction like I'd never seen before. And [then] John sang, 'San Quentin, you're livin' hell to me'…"

Johnny Cash, Folsom State Prison, California, 1968

"It gave everybody the feeling that if they could learn to play 'Folsom Prison Blues', maybe they could stay out of prison."
MERLE HAGGARD

Johnny Cash, Folsom State Prison, California, 1968   99

THE DOORS/JEFFERSON AIRPLANE
THE ROUNDHOUSE, LONDON, 6–7 SEPTEMBER 1968

A disused railway depot may have seemed an unlikely venue for the first visit of America's biggest underground/overground attractions, but The Roundhouse, an airy, circular building, had by 1968 eclipsed UFO as London's leading hippie hangout. It was much bigger, too, and the freaks came out in force for this remarkable double-header, with 10,000 witnessing four concerts over two nights, and many more outside without tickets. Even the Granada TV cameras turned up, eager to catch a rare glimpse of authentic West Coast acid rock, and Doors' frontman Jim Morrison in particular.

Rave magazine dubbed Morrison a superstar (the word had yet to become *de rigueur*) based on reports from America eulogizing the frontman as a new kind of poet-performer, a pop shaman who used sex and highly charged theatrics to devastating effect. A self-styled "erotic politician", Morrison appeared to be some miraculous hybrid of Elvis Presley and a Greek god, and, said guitarist Robbie Krieger, the band's performances were akin to "religious experiences".

Among the congregation in London that autumn were Paul McCartney, Arthur Brown and Traffic, all of whom sat cross-legged in the darkness as the leather-clad Morrison leapt and then fell to the floor, letting out blood-curdling screams before soothing the crowd with a whispered sonnet. Every word, every move, was seemingly filled with significance.

"Jim Morrison lives in exaggerations," enthused Mike Grant in *Rave*. "The dragged-out half stumble and the sloth-like stance on stage, the upturned, pouting face with eyes clenched shut, the ponderous but precise speaking voice…"

The crowd, too, played its part over those four shows, two per night. "One of the best audiences we've ever had," Morrison told Grant after the shows. "Everyone seemed to take it so easy… It stimulated us to give a good performance."

"That was, I think, one of the best concerts I've ever done."
JIM MORRISON

Left: Leather-clad Doors' frontman
Jim Morrison, the self-styled "erotic
politician".

Below: Rob Tyner and MC5
demonstrate their 'White Panther'
politics and tear up Detroit's
Grande Ballroom.

MC5

GRANDE BALLROOM, DETROIT, 30–31 OCTOBER 1968

"We were not effete intellectuals or smartypants artistes like New Yorkers. We were not the laid-back hippies of San Francisco or the plastic culture of Hollywood. This was not über-hip, tailored and Swinging London. This was Detroit. Grimy, sweaty and industrious. With its history of labour struggle and a potent youth culture and anti-war movement, Detroit became the epicentre of radical politics for a generation. The future was now, this was the place, and we were the people to deliver it, mutherfuckers."

Wayne Kramer, *MOJO* magazine, 2003

"We were not effete intellectuals or smarty-pants artistes like in New York." WAYNE KRAMER

MC5, Grande Ballroom, Detroit, 1968

"We were convinced we were the best!"
GINGER BAKER, DRUMMER

Barely two years after they'd formed on the R&B and jazz fringes of the pop world, Cream, rock's first and finest supergroup, disbanded with two sell-out shows at the Albert Hall. No one has ever claimed that the shows were the band's best, but the occasion was so charged with emotion, and the group's split so significant for the future course of rock, that the event remains a rock culture landmark.

This final act had been a long time coming. Cream's forté had been lengthy, loud instrumental battles that invariably pitted all three musicians against each other in a bid to be heard above the resulting mêlèe, but while the jazz-trained rhythm section of Jack Bruce (bass) and Ginger Baker (drums) always managed to lose itself in the rock-based reverie, Eric Clapton soon grew tired of the format. He'd heard The Band's *Music From Big Pink* while on tour in America and, by late spring 1968, hankered for melody and simplicity. Cream, he later insisted, had played itself "into a hole". Then came the news: Cream were to split.

After a summer lay-off, the group took off on one last, highly lucrative US tour before returning to London for the farewell shows, the band's first appearance at home since the start of the year. Clapton, especially, must have felt strangely alone on the Albert Hall stage as he hid behind his floppy fringe, for, despite his misgivings, the virtuoso trio's every move was greeted with howls of approval, a few screams, even tears. The set, which the band had been playing for the past few months, was pleasingly familiar, the soloing more extended than ever. One piece, a 15-minute drum solo titled 'Toad', was less a song than a vehicle for Ginger Baker's stunning dexterity. As Baker pounded away at his double drum kit, sweat dripping from under his headscarf on to his kaftan-style shirt, the crowds whistled their approval.

Clapton's party piece came with the finale, 'Steppin' Out', a lengthy solo guitar break that seemed to confirm all that "Clapton is God" hyperbole of a few years earlier. Jack Bruce, too, played his part, his rasping voice and big fat bass chords serving to enhance the band's bristly virtuosity.

The trio later admitted that they'd been "blown away by the emotion of the audience" – but there was no going back. Oddly, given his musical conversion and perplexed relationship with his superhero status, Clapton – with Baker – subsequently formed a lesser supergroup, Blind Faith. By the early Seventies, though, he'd virtually withdrawn from the rock circus completely.

In May 2005, a reformed Cream returned to the venue for four more sell-out shows, creating even more box-office pandemonium than they did first time round.

Opposite: Jack Bruce, drummer Ginger Baker and guitarist Eric Clapton in rehearsal. The trio show little signs of the acrimony that prematurely pulled the band apart.

CREAM

ROYAL ALBERT HALL, LONDON, 26 NOVEMBER 1968

SET LIST

'WHITE ROOM'
'POLITICIAN'
'I'M SO GLAD'
'SITTING ON TOP OF THE WORLD'
'CROSSROADS'
'TOAD'
'SPOONFUL'
'SUNSHINE OF YOUR LOVE'
'STEPPIN' OUT'

One piece, a 15-minute drum solo titled 'Toad', was less a song than a vehicle for Ginger Baker's stunning dexterity.

John Lennon, Yoko Ono and The Plastic Ono Band

Room 1472, Queen Elizabeth Hotel, Montreal, Canada, 1 June 1969

Today Room 1472, a corner apartment on the 17th floor of the Queen Elizabeth Hotel in downtown Montreal, is known as the John Lennon Suite. Hire the room and you'll be entitled to wear replica John and Yoko pyjamas, enjoy breakfast in bed exactly as they ordered it, and check out with a souvenir print of the lyrics to 'Give Peace A Chance'. Recorded in the suite at the climax of the Lennons' headline-grabbing series of anti-war "bed-ins", the impromptu 'Give Peace a Chance' session was attended by all manner of friends and well-wishers. Nicely mannered English singer Petula Clark was there:

"I was in Montreal, doing a bilingual show in French and English. It was conceived as a way of bringing people together, but it was open warfare in the theatre. Talk about giving peace a chance! I knew John was in town, so I went to see him because I wanted to speak to somebody who had no connection with me, someone I could sit down with and cry and talk to. I had a feeling he would be a kindred spirit, and I was right. He was so sweet. Basically he said, 'Fuck 'em', which I thought was a good piece of advice.

"That first night, there was virtually nobody else there except John and Yoko in bed. When I went back for a second night, the place was full of people, like the Smothers Brothers and Timothy Leary. John was on the huge bed with his acoustic guitar and got us all to sing along. So we did and we all had a nice time. None of us was doing anything particularly naughty. It was just a lovely feeling. I wasn't even aware that we were being filmed or recorded.

"Of course, we all loved the song and were very much in tune with what was being said, of wanting things to be better, to be more in contact with our gentler sides."

"Well, I certainly wasn't stoned or anything. I went along a second night because seeing John had been such a nice experience, and the place turned out to be full of nice people." Petula Clark

VICTOR JARA
ESTADIO CHILE, SANTIAGO, CHILE, JULY 1969

There are few more heroic, or tragic, figures in the history of 20th-century popular music than Victor Jara, the Chilean singer whose songs celebrated the lives of ordinary people and whose murder at the hands of uniformed men has made him a martyr to the cause of human rights.

A leading light of Nueva Cancion, or New Song, a loose aggregation of politically progressive singers in Latin America, Jara came to prominence in July 1969 with a performance that astonished the country, at the same time acting as a barometer for the fast-changing political climate.

The event was billed as the First Festival of New Chilean Song, a discussion forum about the future direction of contemporary Chilean popular music incorporating a song contest. It became, wrote Jara's widow Joan in her book *An Unfinished Song*, a "confrontation" between "the new music, with songs that were critical and committed to revolutionary change, and the 'apolitical' songs which gave the impression that nothing needed changing."

"The authentic revolutionary should be behind the guitar, so that the guitar becomes an instrument of struggle, so that it can also shoot like a gun."
VICTOR JARA

Above: A bouyant Victor Jara is greeted by his wife Joan and other well-wishers after his performance at the First Festival Of New Chilean Song.

Twelve acts, including Victor Jara, then a theatre worker and part-time recording artist, were invited to perform. A more radical group, Quilapayun, were not. Jara, who had written a new song, 'La Plegaria A Un Labrador' ('The Prayer To A Labourer'), for the occasion, invited the banned group to join him on stage, a move the press later denounced as "explosive". Nevertheless, the jury declared Jara's song, a rallying-call to the Chilean peasantry loosely based on the Lord's Prayer, the joint winner.

The crowd in the run-down stadium, situated in the area where Jara grew up, celebrated wildly. "It was a victory for a very profound social movement, with its own cultural expression," Joan Jara remembered. Hugging her husband afterwards, she realized the significance of the victory. "Our lives had reached a turning point," she wrote. "We were irrevocably a part of a process bigger than ourselves."

However, the "time of optimism and commitment" that the Jaras and millions of working people in Chile had been hoping for was short-lived. Soon after Salvador Allende was elected president of Chile, with the full vocal support of Jara and the Nueva Cancion movement, his government was overthrown in a violent coup by the military. Once again, Victor Jara found himself in Estadio Chile. Only this time, on 15 September 1973, he was a prisoner whose hands had been cruelly and deliberately broken. With the taunts of the soldiers echoing around him, the people's musician managed a few bars of the Popular Unity party's campaign song before he was murdered and thrown into a mass grave.

Victor Jara, Estadio Chile, Santiago, 1969

WOODSTOCK ARTS AND MUSIC FAIR
NEAR BETHEL, NEW YORK, 15–17 AUGUST 1969

America was in a mess. Its politicians were being gunned down, its armed forces embroiled in an unjust war on the other side of the world. Civil rights and the so-called youth revolution demanded that the country face up to questions it never wanted to ask. Even in the days before the biggest youth cultural event of the 20th century got underway, the hallowed Hollywood highlife had come under murderous attack from Charles Manson and his gang, erasing much of the optimism of the moon landings the previous month.

On the face of it, Woodstock – three long days and nights of love, peace and music featuring half a million stoned souls and dozens of the era's biggest and best rock, folk and soul acts – provided a respite from America's collective agony, but beyond the gaily painted bodies and the manic, acid-induced grins, the festival wasn't quite the blissful idyll of legend. Rain, bad acid and a traffic gridlock that caused many to miss the festival completely were just some of the more obvious problems that beset the organizers.

No performer epitomized the Janus-faced aspects of the Aquarian age better than Jimi Hendrix, whose torturous, early morning reworking of 'The Star-Spangled Banner' became an imperfectly perfect anthem for a nation virtually at war with itself. One of the most powerful musical statements of modern times, it marked an apotheosis of sorts, a wordless electric storm that remains the most convincing political commentary yet produced within the rock idiom.

The chaotic scheduling meant that by the time Hendrix walked on stage, most of the audience had either gone to sleep or gone home. Ironically, the festival's highest-paid performer was barely part of the Woodstock experience. For those on the ground, the stars of the show were Joe Cocker, for his hand-wringing take on The Beatles' 'With A Little Help From My Friends'; Sly And The Family Stone, whose 'Dance To The Music' got the blissfully stoned crowd on its feet; and Country Joe McDonald, whose 'I-Feel-Like-I'm-Fixin'-To-Die Rag' became the era's cornerstone protest anthem.

"Get off my f**king stage!" The Who's Pete Townshend shows a little peace and love, Mod-style, towards Yippie activist Abbie Hoffman.

Janis Joplin, left, gave the performance of a lifetime.

Opposite, bottom right: Roger Daltrey of The Who.

113

THE ROLLING STONES
ALTAMONT FESTIVAL, CALIFORNIA, 6 DECEMBER 1969

Can one death destroy a dream? When it takes place on the outskirts of hippie haven San Francisco, right under the noses of The Rolling Stones, the answer is inescapably yes. Taking place during the final days of the swinging decade, when youth had seized the wheel and revved off into oblivion, Altamont provided a fitting denouement to a doomed project. Days later, Charles Manson and his so-called "Family" were arrested for the murder of Hollywood star Sharon Tate and her friends. The Beatles fell apart. John Lennon knew the game was up. "The dream is over," he declared.

Hours before the start of the one-day free festival, stage manager Chip Monck was gleefully telling local radio stations:

"This is going to be like a little Woodstock!" But the omens weren't good. The Stones' bad boy reputation had taken on a more serious tone since 1967, with drug busts, rumours of black magic and the death of founder member Brian Jones. Their winter '69 US tour had been dogged by accusations of inflated ticket prices, hence the idea of this fateful, farewell free concert. The aristocrats of the West Coast – Jefferson Airplane, The Grateful Dead, Santana, Crosby, Stills, Nash and Young and The Flying Burrito Brothers were brought on board. So, too, were the local Hell's Angels, ostensibly to police the event.

The moment Mick Jagger stepped off the helicopter, someone punched him in the face, screaming, "I hate you!" Out front, the support acts' performances had been disrupted by fights, freak-outs and the horrific sound of pool cues cracking on craniums. One disgruntled Hell's Angel knocked out Jefferson Airplane singer Marty Balin. When The Grateful Dead arrived and were told what was happening, they turned right back again. The headline act could afford no such luxury. Coming on to face a battered, confused, though in many ways relieved audience, the Stones took to the stage after a lengthy delay. True princes of darkness only come out at night...

The myth machine insists that the sharply dressed 18-year-old black kid Meredith Hunter was fatally stabbed during 'Sympathy For The Devil', but as the tortuous, slow-motion repeats on *Gimme Shelter*, the documentary film of the tour, confirm, the tragedy played out to the slow swagger of 'Under My Thumb'. The footage also reveals that Hunter waved a gun seconds before he was set upon. Days later, The Rolling Stones' new album *Let It Bleed* kicked off with a song that eerily proclaimed: "Murder! It's just a shot away..."

Previous page: Audience member Meredith Hunter waves a gun. Hired as security, a group of Hell's Angels bring him down, and he is stabbed to death in the melee. On stage, just feet away, The Rolling Stones play on oblivious to the tragedy. Welcome to Altamont, the most notorious rock festival of all.

Opposite and right: Just months earlier, on 5 July 1969, Jagger donned his best Ossie Clark frock-coat and the Stones played to a peaceful crowd of 250,000 in London's Hyde Park, a concert that also served as a tribute to the band's founder member Brian Jones, who had been found dead two days earlier.

The Rolling Stones, Altamont Festival, California, 1969

The Politics
Of Flash

HOPES FOR THE NEW "SUPER" DECADE INEVITABLY

RESTED ON THE YOUNG. IT WAS THEY, AFTER ALL, WHO HAD WRENCHED WESTERN CULTURE – WITH THE HELP OF SOME ELEMENTS FROM THE EAST – OUT OF ITS POST-WAR MALAISE AND INTO A MOVING, SHAKING, IF UNCERTAIN FUTURE. BUT, AS THE BEATLES RIGHTLY PREDICTED IN ONE OF THEIR LESSER KNOWN SONGS: IT HAD ALL BEEN TOO MUCH. AFTER THE PARTY – THE LONG, SLOW ROAD TO RECOVERY.

AT THE BEGINNING OF THE 1970S, A NEW BREED OF INTROSPECTIVE SINGER-SONG-WRITERS EMERGED TO PICK UP THE PIECES. NOW, WITH THOSE 'WE SHALL OVERCOME' DEMONSTRATIONS ALL BUT OVER, PERSONAL POLITICS TOOK PRECEDENCE OVER COLLECTIVE ACTION. SURE, THE GREAT ROCK FESTIVALS OF THE LATE '60S CONTINUED WELL INTO THE '70S – IN FACT, THEY GREW BIGGER STILL. BUT, GLASTONBURY ASIDE, THESE WERE NO LONGER MASS DISPLAYS OF COUNTERCULTURAL UNITY BUT SIMPLY ROCK CONCERTS WRIT LARGE. GEORGE HARRISON'S BANGLA DESH FUNDRAISER WAS A VISIONARY ATTEMPT TO BUILD ON ANY RESIDUAL HIPPIE ALTRUISM, THOUGH ITS OBJECTIVE WAS CRUELLY HAMPERED BY GRUBBY REALPOLITIK. BUT THEN, THERE WAS ALWAYS THE MUSIC...

THE ERA'S POLAR OPPOSITES, PROGRESSIVE ROCK AND GLAM ROCK, WERE STRANGELY UNITED IN THEIR DESIRE TO FLOUT CONVENTION AND TAKE OFF ON FANCIFUL FLIGHTS OF EXCESS. WHILE – T. REX'S LEGENDARY SHOWS ASIDE – GLAM WAS ESSENTIALLY A SMALL SCREEN PHENOMENON, PROGMEISTERS SUCH AS ONE-TIME YES KEYBOARD MAN RICK WAKEMAN TOOK ROCK'S CLASSICAL AMBITIONS TO FAINTLY LUDICROUS EXTREMES. THE PRE-PUNK '70S DID YIELD TWO ROCK EVERGREENS, THOUGH, IN DAVID BOWIE AND LED ZEPPELIN. BOWIE'S DECISION TO KILL OFF HIS ZIGGY STARDUST ALTER-EGO ON STAGE TURNED OUT TO BE THE FIRST OF MANY GRAND GESTURES HE'D MAKE DURING HIS CAREER. MEANWHILE, LED ZEPP PUMMELLED THEIR AUDIENCE INTO SUBMISSION BY VIRTUE OF THEIR MUSICAL PROWESS. ONE OF THEIR SONGS, ACTUALLY A LENGTHY SHOWCASE FOR DRUMMER JOHN BONHAM, WAS TITLED 'MOBY DICK'. THAT PRETTY MUCH SUMS UP THE ERA'S SOMETIMES BAFFLING QUEST TO 'GO LARGE'.

This was more Lennon-style primal therapy than love-in.

Melanie was flower power's princess of wails, the original mixed-up, muddled-up hippie chick. Though her contemporaries were Carole King, Carly Simon and Joni Mitchell, her work is surely closer in spirit to Nirvana. Songs of love, loss and loneliness, songs that went soft to loud, tragic to transcendent in seconds, songs strummed with all the earnest ferocity of a punk rocker. A raw, exquisitely voiced maverick for whom mild-mannered, post-hippie moderation simply wasn't on the agenda, Melanie truly let it all hang out.

A staple of all the major rock festivals, Melanie flourished in the company of her own, notoriously zealous fans, who regarded her as a lone beacon of Love Generation innocence and sincerity. At Carnegie Hall, "in the place where I did all my growing up" – and on her 23rd birthday – the audience more than played its part in the ritualized baring of the post-psychedelic soul. It was a night of pin-sharp silences and stage invasions, of nervy monologues and shy giggles. At one point, as the audience's requests reached a high-pitched crescendo, a lone voice piped up: "Do what you wanna do!" Instantly recognizing their thoughtlessness, the crowd let out a huge "Yeah!"

With this kind of adoration, Melanie was regarded by some as impossibly twee – something that also plagued Tyrannosaurus Rex

MELANIE
CARNEGIE HALL, NEW YORK, 3 FEBRUARY 1970

in Britain – but it's a reputation she only partly deserved. For every crowd-pleasing clapalong, such as 'I Don't Eat Animals' and 'Psychotherapy', there were plenty of others that lived up to the singer's bold claim on 'Tuning My Guitar': "I'm gonna sing [about] the life I'm living/And try to ease the pain of all the ones around me..." For sheer musical catharsis, it would be difficult to beat the quivering quartet of songs with which Melanie opened her Carnegie Hall show: 'Close To It All', 'Uptown And Down', 'Mama Mama' ("I fear you reared me wrong"!) and 'The Saddest Thing'. However, it was on 'Tuning My Guitar' that the singer truly hit heroic – and, yes, fabulously histrionic – heights that would put Judy Garland to shame. "I don't care who you are!" Melanie bawled at one point during this extraordinary performance, happily captured on her *Leftover Wine* album.

Isle of White Festival, 1970

ISLE OF WIGHT FESTIVAL

EAST AFTON FARM, FRESHWATER, ISLE OF WIGHT
26–30 AUGUST 1970

The Isle Of Wight, the small island off the south coast of England, had already hosted festivals in 1968 and 1969. The first had been strictly for connoisseurs, a relatively intimate and blissful gathering of the freaks and fans of leading underground acts such as The Crazy World Of Arthur Brown, Tyrannosaurus Rex and, on a rare visit from San Francisco, Jefferson Airplane. The 1969 festival had been a different beast altogether, with The Beatles joining a crowd of 200,000 to witness the return of Bob Dylan after his three-year absence. This time, the event had been organized along the lines of Woodstock, with many acts – including The Who, Richie Havens, Joe Cocker – fresh from Yasgur's Farm and hoping to replicate the vibe. But things didn't always go as planned. Organizational difficulties prevented Dylan from playing longer than an hour, and some of the crowd expressed their displeasure by hurling empty beer cans towards the stage. It was as MC Jeff Dexter recalls an indication of the changing mood at the end of the '60s.

Wednesday: Judas Jump, Kathy Smith, Rosalie Sorrels, David Bromberg, Redbone, Kris Kristofferson, Mighty Baby.

Thursday: Gary Farr, Supertramp, Andy Roberts, Howl, Black Widow, Groundhogs, Terry Reid, Gilberto Gil.

Friday: Fairfield Parlour, Arrival, Lighthouse, Taste, Tony Joe White, Chicago, Family, Procol Harum, The Voices Of East Harlem, Cactus.

Saturday: John Sebastian, Shawn Phillips, Lighthouse, Joni Mitchell, Tiny Tim, Miles Davis, Ten Years After, Emerson, Lake and Palmer, The Doors, The Who, Melanie, Sly And The Family Stone, Tiny Tim.

Sunday: Good News, Kris Kristofferson, Ralph McTell, Heaven, Free, Donovan, Pentangle, Moody Blues, Jethro Tull, Jimi Hendrix, Joan Baez, Leonard Cohen, Richie Havens, Hawkwind.

Opposite (clockwise from top, left): Doors' frontman, Jim Morrison, Keith Emerson from Emerson, Lake and Palmer, Robbie Krieger, Emerson literally on the keyboard.

Below: Jimi Hendrix hitches a ride.

Right: Joni Mitchell, resplendent in yellow.

Opposite: Jimi Hendrix, making his last billed performance on British soil.

A man interrupted Joni Mitchell's performance by grabbing the microphone and announcing, "This is just a hippie concentration camp!" The singer burst into tears.

"People wanted the Sixties to die but I didn't and neither did the majority of the people there. All this stuff about the festival being a disaster is total rubbish. It was probably the first time that proper security was used and some people didn't like that, but there was still a great sense of community, with free macrobiotic food and Release (drug information providers) on hand.

"The fact that the two big-name American acts were disappointing probably discoloured things a bit. The Doors were very low key, especially Jim Morrison. He hid behind his beard and spent most of the time hunched over the microphone.

"Jimi Hendrix had always been the perfect gentleman, but he was odd, in a bit of a state when he arrived. It took him about an hour to get out of his caravan,

and as he was about to go on stage his trousers split and we had to sew them up. Then, when he strapped his guitar on, he realized that the sleeve of his new shirt dangled over the strings. So we pinned them up with safety pins just before I went out to introduce his comeback performance – which turned out to be his last in Britain. It was by no means his best either. I felt a little disappointed and a bit sad.

"Apart from that the festival was phenomenal. The Who were the greatest thing of all. Sly And The Family Stone were fantastic. They came on at dawn, by which time everybody was fast asleep in their sleeping bags, so we had to get everyone to wake up and see them. I didn't sleep for five or six days, and that was largely due to Sly And The Family Stone's 'supplies'. But one of the most astonishing receptions

was for David Bromberg. People were still cheering for him the following day, so we put him on again.

"Joni Mitchell arrived with Neil Young, but when they got off the ferry, they were busted by the police. The manager took the rap, but it freaked them out completely. Neil Young couldn't handle it and went home. Joni was already in a highly emotional state by the time she went on stage, and then her performance was interrupted when that freak came out to talk about free concerts and painting the fences invisible. I'm sure she'll never forget her Isle of Wight performance! But neither will any of us. It was the closest thing we had to Woodstock, the last of the really big classic festivals."

Jeff Dexter, DJ and MC

In 1970, the 'Isle Of Wight Act' was passed by Parliament to ban all future festivals...until 2002.

Isle Of Wight Festival, 1970

GLASTONBURY FESTIVAL
SOMERSET, 20–24 JUNE 1971

Who said the Sixties were over? Timed to coincide with the summer solstice, the second Glastonbury Festival attracted 12, 000 pleasure seekers, who all flocked to the West Country to get naked, get stoned, be spiritual or get laid to the sounds of Arthur Brown's Kingdom Come, David Bowie, Quintessence, Hawkwind, Traffic, Melanie and Fairport Convention. This was certainly the most idyllic of the early Glastonbury Fayres, and as the crowds retired each night to camp in the nearby woods no one gave a moment's thought to the fact that – post Altamont, post-Manson – things might have changed. In this Vale Of Avalon, at least, the Seventies still held much hippie promise.

Glastonbury Festival, 1971

"The schedule was chaotic because there wasn't a tough stage manager. It was unprofessional, but that's the way it was in 1971. And that's why David Bowie ended up going on at 4.30 in the morning instead of before Traffic the previous night. Happily, the sun was just coming up and it was the morning of the solstice. A very special moment."
JOHN COLEMAN, BOOKER

Revellers and performers at Glastonbury enjoy the Somerset summer weather...

Far left: Fairport Convention's Dave Swarbrick.

Above: A made-up member of Arthur Brown's Kingdom Come.

Top left: Magic Michael, who performed naked at the Glastonbury Festival in 1971.

Gong, who played through to the sunset at the Glastonbury Festival.

Family, fronted by singer, Roger Chapman.

"It was the very first ever totally spiritually oriented Festival at Glastonbury and Gong, still an unknown band from France, were destined to play. Despite my having been banned from entering the UK, we made the crossing from Dieppe early one sunny Sunday morning, with an illegal French van and a picture of the Buddha stuck over the ID photo in my passport.

"The site was a series of fields with a cluster of farm buildings at one end and, in the middle distance, a giant pyramid was under careful construction. In the distance could be seen the awe-inspiring presence of Glastonbury Tor.

"Gilli [Gong chanteuse] and I spent our first night on damp ground inside an airless plastic-covered bender that dripped with condensation. I slept superficially, dripping and dipping in and out of consciousness until I became vividly aware of hearing a single voice singing the most beautiful song I could ever possibly imagine. The experience was breathtaking. I gave myself utterly to the beauty of it and it produced in me an ecstatic state like a slow but inevitably building spiritual orgasm. Then it was finished, and I was sitting up wide awake in a sweaty damp plastic tent on the sacred turf of Avalon.

"Later I discovered that David Bowie had been singing and playing at dawn. I wondered who David Bowie was. I later obtained a tape of his dawn serenade but it bore no resemblance to what I had heard. Had I heard him sing and play from out of my body perhaps? It was a mystery...

"Gong were due on mid-afternoon but fate turned it our way. We began in the late afternoon with very few people watching. After ten minutes or so, when we were engrossed in a rapidly mounting rhythmic 'gliss', the generator blew out. By the time we resumed it was that magic sunset time and we were now in the glow of stage lights.

"We had barely restarted when I looked up to see a Pied Piper line of a thousand or so dancing people snaking down the hill to gather in front of the stage, cavorting and rejoicing to the music of this odd French band called Gong. From the glowing cockpit of the pyramid stage this vision was utterly inspiring. We finished with the last rays of sun to the prolonged and heartfelt applause that brings with it the ecstatic tip- tingling sense of soul recognition. I was back in the Land of my Mothers..."

Daevid Allen, Gong

CONCERT FOR BANGLA DESH
MADISON SQUARE GARDEN, NEW YORK, 1 AUGUST 1971

The template for Live Aid, George Harrison's Concert For Bangla Desh differed from its successor on two key counts. Its theme song, simply titled *Bangla Desh* and recorded by the ex-Beatle without a starry cast of thousands in tow, was raw and genuinely moving. Less happily, the several million pounds raised by the project took more than a decade to get through to the people who needed it – by which time it was too late for the hundreds of thousands who'd died in the humanitarian disaster.

This remarkable fund-raising initiative – two concerts, a spin-off triple-LP set and a movie – was put together by Harrison in just five weeks. Ever since playing a rudimentary sitar part on The Beatles' 'Norwegian Wood' in 1965, the guitarist had developed a keen interest in the Indian subcontinent. He'd struck up a close friendship with India's leading sitar player Ravi Shankar, and was the prime mover in The Beatles' sojourn with the Maharishi in the foothills of the Himalayas.

It was Shankar who first alerted Harrison to the crisis in East Pakistan (Bangla Desh). Precipitated by a struggle for independence that, by March 1971, was being savagely crushed by the Pakistan army, millions of impoverished and flood-ravaged people fled across

Concert For Bangla Desh, New York, 1971

Left: A bearded George Harrison and Bob Dylan.

Opposite: George Harrison with Eric Clapton far right.

"I got tired of people saying, 'But what can I do?'"
GEORGE HARRISON

the border into India. Initially, the sitar player had hoped that Harrison might simply lend his support to an evening of Indian music, designed to bring attention – and a little financial relief – to the situation, but the guitarist's imagination was roused.

George Harrison spent much of June and July 1971 on the phone, inviting everyone he knew in the business to join him for what was then an unprecedented initiative in rock music. As Jon Landau later wrote in *Rolling Stone*: "a group of rock musicians recognized, in a deliberate, self-conscious and professional way, that they have responsibilities – and went about dealing with them seriously."

The result was two shows – afternoon and evening – witnessed by a total of 40,000 people, with further funds raised via a spin-off album and full-length concert movie.

More remarkable still was the calibre of the line-up. Bob Dylan, whose attendance no one could predict until he stepped out on stage, made his first public appearance since playing the Isle of Wight Festival in August 1969. Despite his drug habit and consequent problems Eric Clapton made it too, though he later admitted, "I just wasn't there."

Also on board were Harrison's fellow ex-Beatle Ringo Starr, Badfinger, Billy Preston, Leon Russell and a fine supporting cast. And those other two ex-Beatles? While initially supportive, John Lennon eventually declined the invitation, piqued that Yoko had not been asked to appear on stage. And, still smarting from the band's acrimonious split, Paul McCartney stayed at home for fear that the event would further fan those "Beatles To Reform?" rumours.

THE PINK FLOYD
POMPEII, ITALY, 4–7 OCTOBER 1971

The Pink Floyd were always the most austere of the progressive rock groups. Even in 1966, when they were on the cusp of jettisoning R&B for a new psychedelic sound, the quietly spoken quartet hid behind their long fringes and freaky light shows. By 1971, and with the group's main songwriter Syd Barrett long gone, the group had become more anonymous still – only now it was banks of high-tech equipment that separated them from their audiences.

In autumn 1971, and with a view to making a full-length musical film, The Pink Floyd decided to dispense with an audience completely. The idea was to shoot the band in concert but without all the distractions of a college or club gig. So, at the suggestion of director Adrian Maben, the Floyd decamped to an empty Roman amphitheatre amid the ruins of Pompeii, a perfect setting for their lengthy, largely wordless songs. As water bubbled and hot steam rose from Mount Vesuvius nearby, the band's soundscapes, notably 'Echoes' and 'A Saucerful Of Secrets', slowly unfolded with all the epic majesty of grand, post-psychedelic micro-symphonies.

"The fact that it was outdoors, and a bit gritty, gave it a quality that more than made up for the fact that there wasn't an audience. It was a curious, windblown place, though we weren't bothered by the history. When we moved the gear in, I didn't think, 'Here we are one thousand years on, and instead of lions and Christians, The Pink Floyd are here'. We just thought it was an interesting place. I got more sense of where we were when we left the amphitheatre and went to look at some of the ruins outside. Most important of all, it's an astonishingly good performance, one that's lasted really well. It was certainly a very productive period, perhaps the most productive period in the group's history."

Nick Mason, 2005

As they performed their lengthy, largely wordless songs, water bubbled and hot steam rose from Mount Vesuvius nearby.

Above: Roger Waters.

Left: Adrian Maben's film *Pink Foyd Live at Pompeii* shows the ancient amphitheatre slowly fill with a feast of modern-day technology, along with more traditional instruments that Pink Floyd used to achieve their characteristic sound.

It was, some dared insist, a match made in heaven. The Queen Of Soul was going back to church. As the daughter of a gospel-singing mother and a well-known Detroit minister, the Reverend CL Franklin, Aretha Franklin had deep roots in spiritual singing. At 14, she cut her first record, *The Gospel Sound Of Aretha Franklin*, though was soon tempted into the world of secular song by producer John Hammond.

After she made her belated commercial breakthrough in the late '6os, with a series of astonishing, gospel-influenced R&B records, Franklin decided to go back to her roots for what's often been described as one of the finest gospel records ever made. Accompanied by the Southern California Community Choir, led by James Cleveland, an old family friend, she recorded two live shows at the New Temple Missionary Baptist Church in Los Angeles. Inevitably, the bulk of the material consisted of reinterpretations of traditional spiritual material such as 'What A Friend We Have In Jesus', and an extraordinary 10-minute version of 'Amazing Grace' (which gave the resulting album its title). But what made

the performances truly memorable was the way she seamlessly slipped in contemporary pop standards, notably Carole King's 'You've Got A Friend' and Marvin Gaye's 'Wholy Holy', at the same time investing them with new spiritual meaning. "This will go down as Aretha's shining hour," insisted Hammond, even though he no longer worked with her.

"I'm gonna make a gospel record and tell Jesus I cannot bear these burdens alone."
ARETHA FRANKLIN

CAN
COLOGNE SPORTHALLE, GERMANY, 3 FEBRUARY 1972

An unprecedented blur of Karlheinz Stockhausen and James Brown, Jimi Hendrix and The Velvet Underground, Can were the ultimate Krautrock pioneers. "If the Velvets play in a junkyard," enthused *Melody Maker* in 1971, "Can play somewhere more sinister still."

With the band's popularity in their native Germany rising, thanks to some choice film and television soundtracks, Can played

a free, televised show at the massive Sporthalle in Cologne, the city in which they were based. A crowd of 10,000 were spellbound by an extraordinary night of avant-rock that centred on a series of trance-inducing rhythms. As the group extended songs such as 'Spoon' into labyrinthine, compelling creations, full of shifting dynamics, jugglers and acrobats waltzed on and off the stage, adding a slightly surreal edge to the proceedings. None of these

could distract attention from the band's idiosyncratic frontman, however: Japanese singer Damo Suzuki, master of the rag doll dance resplendent in a pink and red velvet jumpsuit. As he yelled from behind his curtain of hair, the rest of the band wove in and out of some of the most innovative and persistent beats ever heard in rock. On this night, as on many others, Can proved they were the true rhythm kings.

Can, Cologne Sporthalle, Germany, 1972

T. REX

It was, the headlines declared, "The Day That Pop Came Back". Not since Beatlemania had Britain witnessed such hysteria as that prompted by Marc Bolan's transformation from poetry-spouting cult hero of the hippie underground to glitter rock superstar. A one-man John, Paul, George and Ringo, Bolan reinvented pop stardom for the post-Beatles generation. Ever since spring 1971, Bolan and his newly expanded and electrified T. Rex had triggered unprecedented levels of fan worship, which reached its apogee at two sell-out shows at Wembley.

Coachloads of teenagers bussed in from all parts of the country jostled with a smattering of inquisitive older Bolan fans, leather-clad Teddy Boys and a platoon of protective parents. There were feather cuts and Bolan perms, Smiley badges and star-shaped patches sewn onto denim. And glitter. Pots of it.

"Are you READY?" roared MC Emperor Rosco. "YEAH!" wailed the 10,000 screamers. When the elf-like Bolan walked onto the stage, the huge hall was transformed as the overwhelmingly teenage-girl audience shrieked in unison. Bolan, his angelic face framed by long, corkscrew hair, played the part of the 20th-century superstar for all it was worth. As his band slipped effortlessly into Bolan boogie mode, he performed like a composite of every rock'n'roll

hero – finger-pointing like Jagger, making Pete Townshend-style leaps and doing the Chuck Berry duckwalk across the stage.

"Marc Bolan certainly holds a frightening amount of power," remarked *Sounds'* Steve Peacock, but then so did the fans. "Without them, I'm just a poet," Bolan acknowledged. "With them I'm a rock'n'roll star."

Despite his larger-than-life persona, Marc Bolan seemed to connect with his fans like no other. Showy yet poetic and sensitive, he could leave a Wembley audience spellbound with a mid-set acoustic interlude, accompanying his delicate warbling voice with a slightly out-of-tune acoustic guitar. No one cared, because when Bolan sang his self-mythologizing 'Cosmic Dancer', his fans felt as if they were in the presence of a latter-day deity. So, too, did Beatles drummer turned filmmaker Ringo Starr, who was at the front with his movie camera shooting the event for the *Born To Boogie* film.

"I was just gawking, cos I loved him up there," Ringo enthused. "He's exciting and just to see all those people dressed like him again...We were all trying to deny it but...it is showbiz. When we get up there on stage, we're just the same as Hedy Lamarr."

"We've done in a year what took The Beatles four years," Bolan bragged. It certainly felt that way back in spring 1972.

"He was the first one, whatever anybody says, to get the kids back out of their seats, jumping up and screaming about..."
RINGO STARR

T. Rex, Empire Pool, Wembley, 1972

Top: Percussionist Mickey Finn with T. Rex bassist Steve Currie.

Bottom right: Bolan backstage.

"Fanmania reminiscent of The Beatles' touring days in 1964 and 1965 returned to London on Saturday…" Melody Maker

ALICE COOPER

EMPIRE POOL, WEMBLEY, LONDON, 30 JUNE 1972

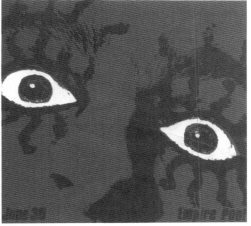

Debuting in New York on 1 December 1971, Alice Cooper's *Killer* show was a shocking piece of rock theatre that, said the singer, was a "direct product of television and movies and America". With the band's latest single 'School's Out' about to rip up the British charts, the horror show – complete with live boa constrictor, decapitated dolls and fully functioning guillotine – bowed out with a headline-grabbing performance in London. Teenage superfan Simone Stenfors was there:

"I was the biggest Alice Cooper fan on the planet. Everything about the group was completely different. It was a horror movie. It wasn't nice like everything else was. Like Captain Beefheart and Frank Zappa, it was music for freaks. But around the time of the concert, they appeared on *Top Of The Pops* and there were all these Alice Cooper lookalikes in the audience. Screaming girls down the front, too. That pissed me off a bit because they were *my* group! I didn't like it that they'd got so huge.

"Our seats were right at the back, so while the support band were playing, me and my girlfriend talked these two guys into selling us their tickets, which were about ten rows from the front. By the time Roxy Music had finished playing, all my friends were down there too, and I was sitting on this guy's lap right next to the catwalk. So when Alice stepped onto it and sat down, I was level with him. When he sang 'Dead Babies', and ripped the clothes off the doll, he was staring right into my face.

"I don't know if it was scary. I was a young teenager and just caught up in it all. No one had seen a performance like that back then. He had the snake for 'Is It My Body', the gallows for 'Killer' and all these blood pellets. There was this rumour going around that he nearly got decapitated. I suppose that was all hype and hearsay, but the audience was made up of 15- to 18-year-olds, and it certainly impressed us.

"When Alice sang 'School's Out' near the end of the set, he threw gladioli into the audience. He put one in my hand, and when I got home, I lovingly placed it in a glass of water. My mother threw it out. She didn't realize how much it meant."

"It's really nothing more than a mirror which I place in front of an audience to reflect the very darkest side of human nature."

ALICE COOPER TO ROY CARR, *MUSIC SCENE*, 1972

IGGY AND THE STOOGES
LA SCALA, KINGS CROSS, LONDON, 15 JULY 1972

"We'd heard all the stories – about how he'd flash his penis, smear himself with peanut butter, cut himself, jump into the audience and crowd surf across a sea of hands. But Iggy didn't do any of that. He didn't need to. It was his presence that was so potent. He was not like anything we'd seen before in London. He had this aura of menace, like something that was caged and very angry, something dreamed up by Carl Jung, something that had dropped in from the depths of your psyche. Remember, this was years before the Sex Pistols.

"Everyone was seated. There were no more than a few hundred there. And the set was short, probably no more than 40 minutes. But the audience were stunned. They just sat there and wondered what the fuck to make of it all, this freak show which was riveting and had a real threatening edge to it. I'd not experienced anything so unprecedented since seeing The Pink Floyd

before they were famous. It was like art, showing you another way of looking at things, of feeling things.

"To this day, Iggy is still the definition of punk. Johnny Rotten was a master of irony, it was all in the mind. But Iggy was primal. He got right deep into the gut. A lot of it was to do with his physicality. Maybe it was that teetering on the edge of self-destruction thing. Visually he had this destructive sexual thing about him, too. So did Jim Morrison, but Iggy went way beyond Morrison, beyond Jagger, too. You never felt that Mick was gonna go down in flames.

"People always ask me about this gig. Perhaps because so much else was going on. [Bowie's] *Ziggy Stardust* had just been released, Lou [Reed] was in town, and I think had played the same venue the night before, and I'd taken that fellatio shot of David [Bowie] and Mick [Ronson] a month or so earlier. It all seemed to happen within

a very short period of time. I think we all thought we were living out the last days of rock'n'roll. That was the romantic fantasy that fuelled this whole thing. There was a certain manic desperation about it. The resonance of what the 'terrible trio' – David, Lou and Iggy – did at that time has turned out to be massive. It had nothing to do with The Beatles, the Stones or Dylan. It was the birth of a new sensibility.

"Glam was all about looking fabulous, and punk was all about looking raw. And Iggy, with his silver hair and silver trousers, is the perfect avatar for both glam and punk. That show was totally unique in more ways than it simply being the only time the Stooges ever played Britain. We're still only coming to terms with its importance."

Mick Rock, photographer

150   Iggy And The Stooges, La Scala, London, 1972

Iggy And The Stooges, La Scala, London, 1972　　151

Opposite: Chuck Berry, doing his famous duckwalk for the Wembley crowd.

The London Rock'n'Roll Show, Wembley Stadium, 1972

The London Rock'n'Roll Show

Wembley Stadium, London, 5 August 1972

At almost the moment flower power wilted, and with it the wilder excesses of cultural experimentation, Britain experienced a rock'n'roll revival. Bill Haley And The Comets toured to a heroes' welcome, The Beatles sang the Fifties-inspired 'Get Back' and plans were made for a huge rock'n'roll revival show in London. Four years later, at the height of revivalist glam rock, the rockers' Woodstock finally took place.

A crowd of 50,000 arrived for what was the first major rock show at Wembley Stadium. A motley mix of magnificently quiffed Teds in drapes and creepers, rockers in oil-ruined Levis and studded leather, and a smattering of flat caps and dour, anti-fashion threads, the gathering marked a unique moment in British pop. It was as if the Sixties had never happened.

If the audience represented an unholy alliance of future-fearing forces, on stage any apparent unity was similarly fragile. Detroit rock'n'roll radicals MC5 banged out their customary ramalama dressed in silver spacesuits and gold lamé, and with hippie-style hair. This was greeted with a hail of Coke cans, wine bottles and eerie silences at the end of songs, punctuated by the occasional slow handclap. Another hairy, Wizzard's rock'n'roll-obsessed frontman Roy Wood, didn't fare much better.

Even bona fide rock'n'roll legends didn't necessarily meet the exacting standards of the assembled throng. Little Richard, who punctuated his set with rants about Black Power while stripping off in characteristic ultra-camp fashion, was as much abused as he was adored. The similarly flamboyant Screamin' Lord Sutch, who was brought on stage in a coffin, appeared to strike the right chord by bringing on a bevy of bikini-clad dancers and a stripper.

Headliner Chuck Berry – duckwalking in a psychedelic shirt – stole the day, confirming his reputation as the man who single-handedly defined the sound of rock'n'roll. Bill Haley, still sporting the kiss-curl hair, pristine white jacket and outsize guitar from his mid-Fifties heyday, got the Teds stomping hard with 'Rock Around The Clock'. Looking mean and leaping atop his piano was Jerry Lee Lewis – the Killer – his cold stare no less menacing than rogue elements within the crowd.

Lurking and smirking in his leopard-skin cap and drape suit that day was future Sex Pistols manager Malcolm McLaren. The proprietor of noted Teds fashion emporium Let It Rock was there to flog T-shirts that featured the slogan Vive Le Rock over a photograph of Little Richard. Five years later, McLaren had become the most notorious man in Britain, punk's Svengali figure and – ironically – a hate figure for the Teds.

"The few acts on the bill...pushing rock'n'roll ahead were either received with stony silence or with boos, catcalls, V-signs...and, at one point, with a hail of beer cans and bottles. The MC5, who played some searing music, were forced off by howls of derision..." Martin Hayman, *Sounds*, August 1972

DEEP PURPLE
OSAKA AND TOKYO, JAPAN, 15–17 AUGUST 1972

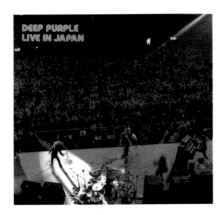

As 'Child In Time', Deep Purple's brooding, intermittently explosive epic picked up pace, bassist Roger Glover looked out from the stage as over 10,000 fans began to sing along. He was on the other side of the globe, in Japan, still a relatively rare stopping-off point for major acts. The crowd must have had little idea what they were singing along to, but Glover, then part of one of the world's most successful rock machines, was deeply moved. "If ever there was a moment when I was proud to be in Deep Purple, that was it," he said later.

Deep Purple spent 44 weeks on the road during 1972, an extraordinarily hectic schedule that in effect broke the band, for by the following spring, both Glover and vocalist Ian Gillan had quit. However, the short, three-date tour of Japan, originally scheduled for May 1972 but delayed by three months to accommodate more American dates, yielded what has often been described as the ultimate live hard rock album.

The band, their reputation sealed by the success of *Deep Purple In Rock*, *Fireball* and *Machine Head*, were by now a fearsome in-concert attraction, up there alongside Led Zeppelin and The Who. Supremely confident, their forte was stretching out album tracks such as 'Space Truckin'' and 'Highway Star' into labyrinthine epics. Yet in dazzling audiences with their virtuoso displays, Purple nevertheless kept a keen distance from their indulgent progressive rock contemporaries, not least by making sure that these thrillingly stretched versions were often performed at breathtaking velocity.

The result of this extraordinary trio of gigs was an explosive double live album, *Made In Japan*. "It's the best those numbers have ever been played on record," said Ian Gillan at the time, confirming also that the band's natural home was the stage not the studio. *Rolling Stone* magazine described it as "Purple's definitive metal monster". The band went home and wrote a song about it, 'Woman From Tokyo' ("Fly into the rising sun/Faces smiling everyone"), and it has since become one of the most successful live albums ever, thanks in no small part to the white-hot rapport between audience and band that elevates the record.

WATTSTAX
MEMORIAL COLISEUM, LOS ANGELES, 20 AUGUST 1972

Almost exactly seven years on from the Watts riots, in which 34 people died in the almost exclusively black district of South Los Angeles, came the nearest thing to the black community's Woodstock. A collaboration between the Watts Summer Festival (set up in the aftermath of the violence) and Memphis-based Stax Records, Wattstax was a loud, proud celebration of LA's Afro-American community that became a top-selling record, a full-length feature film and a unique snapshot of a culture in transition.

No one caught the mood better than Jesse Jackson, who MC'd the day-long event. "We've gone from 'Burn, baby, burn' to 'Learn, baby, learn'," he declared as the show got underway at 3pm on a hot summer's afternoon, before calling on the 100,000-strong audience to repeat the mantra "I Am Somebody!"

Everybody was somebody that day, but none more so than Isaac Hayes, fresh from his Oscar-winning triumph with *Shaft*. Flinging off his cape to reveal a gold chain vest, and performing in front of lights that repeatedly flashed "SHAFT" and "BLACK MOSES", Hayes' flamboyant performance capped a day of pride and joyous exhibitionism.

Hayes was undoubtedly the man of the moment, but Wattstax heaved with living legends. Rufus Thomas had the crowd on its feet and doing the funky chicken, The Staple Singers shone a light of spirituality with their uplifting gospel harmonies, while The Emotions, The Bar-Kays, Eddie Floyd, Carla Thomas and guitarist Albert King brought a range of styles to the event. When Kim Weston, who'd opened the show with a coolly received 'Star-Spangled Banner', returned to close the night with the black solidarity anthem 'Lift Every Voice And Sing', the entire audience was on its feet and as one.

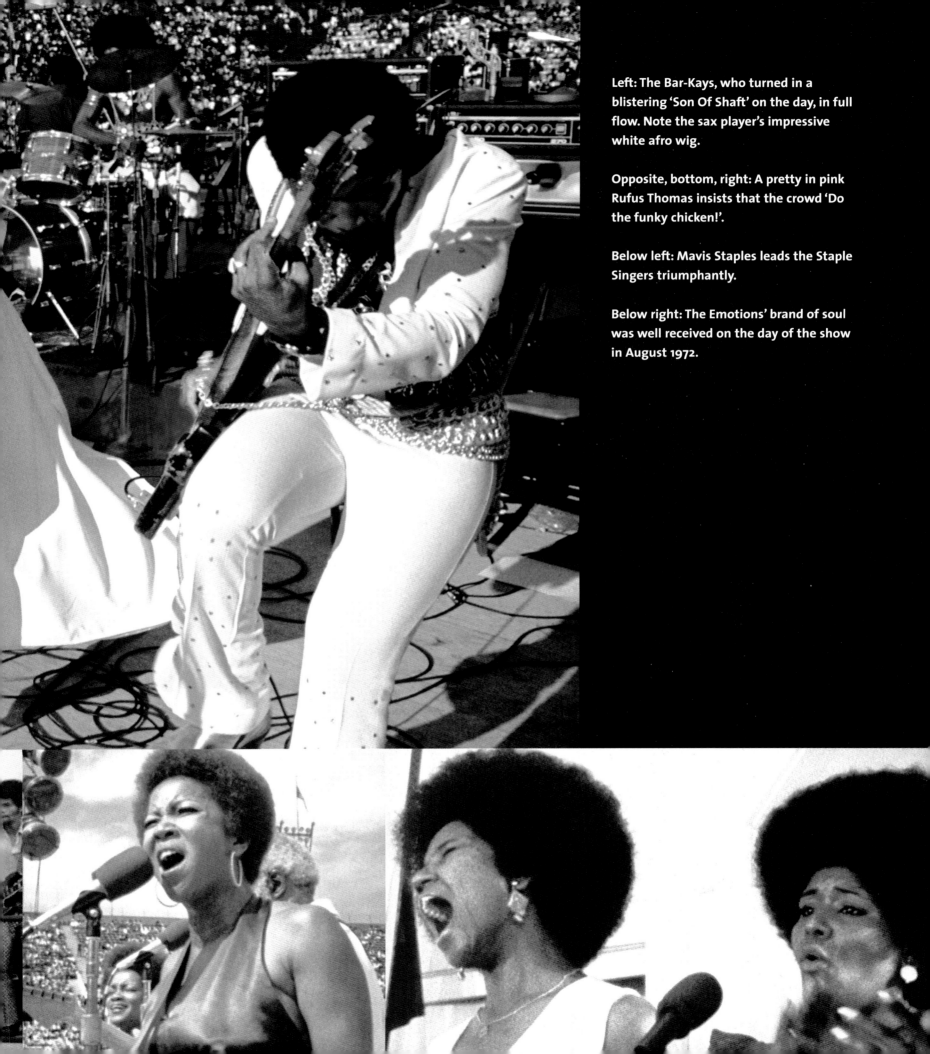

Left: The Bar-Kays, who turned in a blistering 'Son Of Shaft' on the day, in full flow. Note the sax player's impressive white afro wig.

Opposite, bottom, right: A pretty in pink Rufus Thomas insists that the crowd 'Do the funky chicken!'.

Below left: Mavis Staples leads the Staple Singers triumphantly.

Below right: The Emotions' brand of soul was well received on the day of the show in August 1972.

ERIC CLAPTON
THE RAINBOW, LONDON, 13 JANUARY 1973

Rock stars doing disappearing acts wasn't entirely new by the early Seventies. Bob Dylan conveniently used a motorcycle accident as a ruse to fade away for three years in the late Sixties. The Beatles escaped the pressures of post-Sgt Pepper fame by retreating to a hideaway in the foothills of the Himalayas with their spiritual guru the Maharishi. But Eric Clapton's self-imposed exile from pop fame – which, at its height, had seen "Clapton is God" graffiti spray-painted all over London – had led him straight into a career- and life-threatening drug habit. "I had to go into the darkness," he explained later.

Friend and fellow guitarist The Who's Pete Townshend, who'd been deeply affected by the recent deaths of Brian Jones and Jimi Hendrix, had seen the warning signs. So, too, had Lord Harlech, aristocrat father of Clapton's girlfriend Alice Ormsby-Gore. Together the pair hatched a plan to get Clapton working again.

After little more than a week of rehearsals at Ronnie Wood's Hampton Court home, Eric Clapton emerged with an all-star band featuring Jim Capaldi, Steve Winwood, Ric Grech and Rebop alongside Townshend and Wood. George Harrison and Ringo Starr, Paul and Linda McCartney, Elton John, Joe Cocker and Jimmy Page were just a few of the famous faces in the audience, together with a couple of thousand fans, all eager for a rare glimpse of the guitar guru.

Because of the precarious nature of Clapton's condition, the makeshift band was privately dubbed The Palpitations, due to a suspicion that the guitarist might bottle the performance. It was a close thing: Clapton arrived just one minute before he was due on stage.

Bearded and a little heavier than when he was last seen in public, he opened with 'Layla' and everyone's nerves quickly steadied. It was a historic show, but not, reckoned the guitarist, necessarily a classic one. "Well under par," Clapton admitted later. A surfeit of guitarists took the edge off his playing, though less remarked upon at the time was the change in his voice, which had acquired a new soulful edge – but everyone was just simply delighted to have him back.

Elvis Presley had made his television comeback in 1968. He'd also perfected a new supper-club style act and cracked Las Vegas. He was the biggest star in the world, but neither he nor his manager Colonel Tom Parker had any desire to spend a minute beyond the borders of the United States. Hence this technological breakthrough – the first live concert performance via satellite – that enabled Presley to reach a global market with just one two-hour show.

Elvis in Hawaii notched up better viewing figures than the moon landings. In Japan, an astonishing 98 per cent of the television audience was transfixed by the sight of a 38-year-old American man in an laundry-white jumpsuit, emblazoned with an American eagle, belting out a mix of uptempo rock'n'roll songs and lachrymose ballads all the way from Polynesian paradise. It was a spectacle guaranteed to write itself instantly into the

Elvis in Hawaii notched up better viewing figures than the moon landings.

4 DAYS' REHEARSAL
23 SONGS
25 POUNDS LOST IN BUILD-UP TO THE SHOW
8,000 IN THE HONOLULU INTERNATIONAL CENTER
$85,000 RAISED FOR LOCAL CANCER FUND
$1M PAID TO ELVIS PRESLEY
$2.5M PRODUCTION COSTS
1.1 BILLION VIEWERS WORLDWIDE

history books, but few were aware of the private hell that Presley was making public in songs such as 'You Gave Me A Mountain', 'It's Over' and Hank Williams' 'I'm So Lonesome I Could Cry' – "The saddest song I ever heard," the King told his global parish. Months earlier, Elvis had lost his wife and daughter to another man. Even in the company of over a billion people, Elvis Presley was still stuck on Lonely Street...

Elvis Presley, International Center, Honolulu, 1973

DAVID BOWIE AND THE SPIDERS FROM MARS

HAMMERSMITH ODEON, LONDON, 3 JULY 1973

When Bowie broke big the previous summer, there'd been a whiff of debate about his sexuality, but little confusion about his identity. By the time his 18-month Ziggy Stardust tour rolled into Hammersmith Odeon on 3 July 1973, fans and friends alike had succumbed to the extraordinary power of the persona he'd created – and so, too, had Bowie himself. "It was so much easier for me to live within that character," he remarked later. Ziggy had to go.

Unbeknown to everyone except his manager Tony DeFries and guitarist Mick Ronson, Bowie had a dramatic announcement to make at the concert, something that would top even the drama of the previous year that had seen him leapfrog Marc Bolan to become pop's first sultan of strange.

In an era of grand gestures, Bowie's surprise decision, uttered before a climactic and entirely fitting 'Rock'n'Roll Suicide', eclipsed them all. At the peak of his fame, here was David Bowie spectacularly announcing his retirement, prompting gasps of "No-o-o-o!" from the crowd. But if Bowie thought he was banishing Ziggy Stardust, he was wrong. "I wasn't getting rid of him at all," he said years later. "In fact, I was joining forces with him. The doppelganger and myself were starting to become one and the same person. And then you start on this trail of chaotic psychological destruction."

"BOWIE QUITS!" screamed the headlines, but though the concert marked the end of an era, it was by no means the end of Bowie. Less than two months later, the singer was back on stage, filming a television special at the Marquee Club.

BOWIE'S BOMBSHELL...

"Everybody. This has been one of the greatest tours of our lives. I would like to thank the band. I would like to thank our road crew. I would like to thank our lighting people...Of all of the shows on this tour, this particular show will remain with us the longest because...not only is it the last show of the tour, but it's the last show that we'll ever do. Thank you."

A Spider Speaks...

Spiders drummer Woody Woodmansey on his last night with Bowie:

Expect anything out of the ordinary?
No, not particularly.

The crowd. More hysterical than normal?
Always hysterical!

The performance?
Very emotional. It was the last gig of the tour.

Did you hear David's announcement?
Yes.

What was said in the dressing room afterwards?
Couldn't possibly repeat that.

How did you feel next day?
Pretty good. I got married.

When did the penny drop that the Spiders were no more?
When my drumstick missed David's head on stage!

David Bowie And The Spiders From Mars, 1973

"I thought they were the best shows that we've ever put on in England." JOHN BONHAM, 1975

LED ZEPPELIN
EARL'S COURT, LONDON, MAY 1975

For five nights in May 1975, and to a total audience of 85,000 people, Led Zeppelin confirmed their status as the biggest and most musically significant band of the Seventies. Everything about the Earls Court shows suggested largesse, from the huge video backdrops to the towering dual presence of singer Robert Plant and guitarist Jimmy Page, from the breadth of musical styles covered during the three-and-a-half hour sets to the awesome majesty of the Led Zepp sound. Those who spent 24 hours queuing for tickets, which sold out in an amazing four hours, had their devotion justly rewarded.

What they witnessed was, insisted *Melody Maker*'s Michael Oldfield, "the definitive rock performance". The set was drawn from all parts of the group's six-year-plus career and, in encompassing so many styles, seemed to encapsulate just about everything that had happened in rock since the beat-group era. Consummate musicians every one, Messrs Plant, Page, Jones and Bonham were able to move effortlessly from robust blues-rock

('Dazed And Confused') to harmony-led material ('Tangerine'), gargantuan rock excess (the 'Moby Dick' drum solo) to progressive rock ('No Quarter'), and post-hippie pastorals ('Going To California') to era-defining epics such as 'Stairway To Heaven' and 'Kashmir'.

'Kashmir', the centrepiece of the band's latest chart-topping album *Physical Graffiti*, suggested that, far from sliding into the mid-decade torpor that was adversely affecting so many of their contemporaries, Led Zeppelin were still in peak condition. But events were soon to overtake them. In August that year, Robert Plant was badly injured in a car accident in Rhodes, which curtailed the group's activities. By the time the band returned in 1977 for a huge, though problem-beset, tour of the States, punk had happened and Led Zeppelin, the band that had once owned the decade, were no longer in the driving seat. Time, of course, has since changed all that: 30 years on, the legend of Led Zeppelin packs no less a punch than it did at the time of their short, explosive Earl's Court residency.

Led Zeppelin, Earls Court, London, 1975

Having already unfurled two progressive rock extravaganzas, *The Six Wives Of Henry VIII* and *Journey To The Centre Of The Earth*, Rick Wakeman decided that his third epic, *Myths And Legends Of King Arthur And His Knights Of The Round Table*, merited an outlandish and quite probably preposterous stage show:

"The management wanted to put the King Arthur shows on at the Albert Hall. I wanted Wembley, but because there was this big ice show happening a week or so later, they told me it was impossible. I was fuming, so I met up with Chris Welch at *Melody Maker* and announced that I was gonna perform *King Arthur*...at Wembley...on ice! The paper made it a big story, so there was no going back.

"I put in my own money, which gave me total control, and I wanted the best. Most of the skaters were flown in from around the world. We flew the PA – the first to be net-hung – in from America and put together a huge cast. I had a 45-piece

RICK WAKEMAN

orchestra, 48 singers in two choirs, 50 skaters, 50 knights, a seven-piece band, a narrator and heaven knows what else.

"It was fun, but it wasn't without its problems! One night, as soon as I walked on, my cape got caught on one of the elevated keyboards, and I was left hanging in mid-air. It was only the first number and I had to go off, dazed, while trying to negotiate the ice.

"Then there was the dry ice, which was hard to control on that scale. On the first night, it was hovering nicely at knight level, when we noticed it rising. And continuing to rise. No one was able to turn the machines off, and by the end of 'Lady Of The Lake', the dancing Guinevere had disappeared completely. So had the lower tier of the orchestra and the first tier of the auditorium. It was like looking out of an aeroplane window.

"That was the 'cloud night'. Then there was the night the knight committed suicide. In the final battle, there were 25 knights opposite each other, poised to simultaneously kill each other and disappear into the dry ice. On the last night, I was told that one of the knights was ill. 'Doesn't matter,' I said. 'There are loads of knights.' But of course when we finished the piece, there was this one knight still looking around for someone to kill him. The conductor looked at me helplessly. But this guy was brilliant. He wandered aimlessly, then had a stroke of genius and committed suicide. Pure entertainment!"

"An evening that literally had to be seen to be believed." PAUL GAMBACCINI, *ROLLING STONE*, 1975

Around the time of his bizarre King Arthur extravaganzas, Rick Wakeman employed a drinks roadie who'd hide under the Hammond organ and pour out pints of beer and shots of whisky for his caped employer.

The Angry
Brigade

IT IS ONLY WITH HINDSIGHT THAT THE EMERGENCE OF PUNK HAS A WHIFF OF INEVITABILITY ABOUT IT. FROM THE VELVETS TO THE VOIDOIDS, VIA THE STOOGES AND BOWIE'S OUTRÉ GLAM — THE LINEAGE DOES APPEAR TO BE RELATIVELY STRAIGHT-FORWARD. REAL HISTORY, THOUGH, IS RARELY THAT NEAT AND TIDY. FOR A GENERATION OF TEENAGERS FAR TOO YOUNG TO HAVE EXPERIENCED THE WATERSHED MOMENT OF BEATLEMANIA AND THE ENSUING BEAT BOOM, PUNK WAS WHOLLY UNPRECEDENTED, VERY MUCH IN THE NOW AND WITH ORIGINS THAT SEEMED INDISTINCT AT BEST. IT WAS NOTHING LESS THAN THE SHOCKINGLY RUDE HOWL OF THE CULTURALLY DISPOSSESSED THAT TURNED THE ROCK WORLD UPSIDE DOWN.

AFTER PUNK, EVERYTHING WAS DIFFERENT. THE SOUND, THE LOOK, EVEN THE VERY PACE OF LIFE HAD CHANGED. AND FOR THE FIRST TIME IN A GENERATION, ROCK SPOKE TO ITS AUDIENCE ONCE AGAIN. THE OLD PROGRESSIVE ERA CONCERT SPECTACULARS HARDLY VANISHED OVERNIGHT. IN FACT, AS A LARGE RUMP OF PUNK-PHOBIC ROCK BUFFS RUSHED TO FIND SOMETHING WITH A BIT OF CULTURAL CERTAINTY ABOUT IT, MANY 'OLD FARTS' FLOURISHED. BUT THE NATURE OF CONCERT-GOING HAD BEEN OVERTURNED AS THE PUB AND CLUB CIRCUIT, PRIZED OPEN BY PUB ROCK IN THE MID-'70S, OFFERED A MORE HIGHLY CHARGED ENVIRONMENT IN WHICH THE ICONOCLASTS COULD FLOURISH. MEDIAEVAL KNIGHTS JOUSTING ON ICE WERE SHOULDER-CHARGED OFF THE FRONT PAGES BY A NEW GENERATION OF MAD-EYED KNAVES, ON THEIR FEET AND JOSTLING FOR PRIME POSITION AT THE FRONT OF THE STAGE. AND, AS EVERYONE RUSHED TO FORM BANDS, SOMETIMES THEY FOUND THEMSELVES ON IT.

PLASTIC PEOPLE
FESTIVAL OF THE SECOND CULTURE, BOJANOVICA, CZECHOSLOVAKIA, 21 FEBRUARY 1976

Few concerts can genuinely be said to have sparked a revolution. This one did. The Plastic People Of The Universe, who had taken their name from a Frank Zappa song and their inspiration from Andy Warhol and The Velvet Underground, had been a thorn in the Czech authorities' side since 1968. Refusing the so-called "normalization" process initiated after the Soviet invasion earlier that year, their "Happening"-style performances were viewed with suspicion by the authorities and, by the start of 1970, their

professional status was revoked. The Plastic People were duly forced underground, their music denounced as "morbid", their cultural position "negative".

This only hardened the band's resolve and, as their music became darker and more avant-garde, their infrequent attempts to perform met with even more opposition. When police attacked and broke up a 1,000-strong crowd that had gathered before a secret show in the small town of Budovice in 1974, main man Ivan

Left: The Plastic People Of The Universe, led by guitarist Milan Hlavsa, genuinely suffered for their art – but their work helped hasten the demise of a culturally bankrupt state.

Above: The arrival of sax player and songwriter Vratislav Brabenec in the early '70s coincided with the group venturing further away from the mainstream.

Jirous organized the First Music Festival of the Second Culture (the First Culture being the despised art sanctioned by the totalitarian regime). This determined show of strength took place on 1 September that year.

However, the critical date in the history of the Plastic People and, arguably, in the story of the Czech Republic is 21 February 1976. On that day, a Second Music Festival of the Second Culture (alias Druha Kultura) took place, this time in Bojanovica. On this occasion, the authorities did not let it pass without action. Within a month, over two dozen musicians had been arrested, their instruments, books and papers seized. Six months later, the Plastic People and their fellow "anti-socials" were on trial, and prison sentences were duly handed out to four of them. Regarded as the chief "disturber of the peace", Jirous was given

an 18-month jail sentence.

The trial prompted much outrage, both in Czechoslovakia and abroad. One particularly vocal critic was playright Vaclav Havel, a driving force behind Charter 77, the human rights movement that provided the blueprint for the Velvet Revolution that eventually put an end to Soviet-dominated rule in 1989. Havel's claim that the Plastic People were merely exercising "life's intrinsic desire to express itself freely" landed him in jail, too. A decade later, though, he was the first president of the Czech Republic – and the Plastic People Of The Universe had become (reluctant) heroes. It's no coincidence that two of the first visitors to the newly liberated country were the band's original inspirations, Frank Zappa and The Velvet Underground's Lou Reed.

PATTI SMITH
THE ROUNDHOUSE, LONDON, 16–17 MAY 1976

Patti Smith's *Horses* sounded like nothing else. A debut album instantly compared to all the great rock'n'roll debut LPs, it fused art and energy in a way that was virtually incomprehensible in rock's otherwise bloated and increasingly superfluous mid-Seventies. Six months later, Smith's self-styled "three-chord rock merged with the power of the word" rolled into London, where a thrill-starved minority was eager to catch at first-hand what had been happening in New York clubs such as CBGB's and Max's Kansas City.

High on rebellion, higher still on rock'n'roll mythology, Patti Smith was the one who stopped the rot. Misleadingly described as "the new Bruce Springsteen", this electrifying performer, who packed out The Roundhouse on two consecutive nights, was a far more incendiary figure. Spearheading what she called "the fight against fat and Roman satisfaction", Patti was lean and mean, her pasty complexion, sunken cheeks and fabulously androgynous look signifying something different altogether. She also addressed the 50 per cent of the population that had been largely ignored by the rock world. "There weren't many female singers around like Patti Smith," says Pauline Murray, who went on to front punk band Penetration. "I mean, she was really weird. Before her, there were only those country music crossover singers like Tanya Tucker." Future members of all-women punk bands The Slits and The Raincoats first crossed paths at Patti's Roundhouse gigs.

Patti Smith and her group opened their set with a mildly obscure Velvet Underground song, 'We're Gonna Have A Real Good Time Together', a glorious affirmation of the turn towards the revived three-chord aesthetic, but at least as important was her look. "Red bandana tied at her throat," noted *Sounds'* Giovanni Dadamo, "one open black smock with embroidered birds on the back, over a muddy thigh-length skirt, over a T-shirt and sausage-skin blue jeans tucked into low-lace boots." Plus, to top it off, one of her characteristic "I'm Your Fan" T-shirts, this particular one declaring "Love Rastafari And Live".

Ever the rock'n'roll obsessive, she dedicated 'Land' to Keith Relf, the recently departed ex-Yardbirds singer, claiming bizarrely that he was "the man who invented feedback". She ended the show with a reworking of the old R&B hit 'Time Is On My Side', popularized by The Rolling Stones, which she customized with her own "Tick, tock, fuck the clock..." intro.

"When I first sat down at my typewriter," concluded an exhausted Dadamo, "all I wanted to do was type 'it was great' over and over again until I fell asleep. It was great."

Left: Patti Smith and her group rewrote the rock'n'roll rulebook with an artful take on garage rock.

Opposite: A confirmed rockaholic, Smith was renowned for wearing T-shirts declaring her devotion to The Rolling Stones and reggae legends.

"Together they achieved an inspired performance of Minimalist Art."

MICHAEL WATTS, *MELODY MAKER*

Patti Smith, The Roundhouse, London, 1976

THE RAMONES
THE ROUNDHOUSE, LONDON, 4 JULY 1976

Patti Smith, New York's rising anti-star high on the rebellion of Rimbaud and reggae, had made her British debut at The Roundhouse a few weeks earlier, but when The Ramones came to town, there were no poetry readings or Keith Richards T-shirts. Young, loud and spotty, The Ramones grunted petulantly into their mics, bashed out their set at superfast speed, pausing only to take off their leather jackets, and quit the stage to a beery chorus of cheers after just half an hour. It was, reckoned Max Bell in the following week's *Melody Maker*, nothing short of "Moronrock," and he – like most everyone in the 1,500-strong crowd – approved. "Moronrock" as a description of the oncoming sonic storm never did catch on, but the style and sound unveiled by The Ramones at the Roundhouse certainly did.

Virtually everyone who ended up in punk bands was there, gobsmacked as The Ramones revelled in their unvarnished white trash status. Simplicity was the key: matching names (Joey Ramone, Dee Dee Ramone and so on), identikit street style, songs that blurred into one another. Costumed in cheap sneakers, torn-up drainpipe denims and tight-fitting T-shirts, The Ramones struck legs-apart-knees-bent poses, their gaunt, unsmiling faces revealing no emotion whatsoever. Bowl-headed bassist Dee Dee Ramone, "possibly the most half-witted specimen" Max Bell had ever seen on a stage, played so fiercely that he cut his finger. Somewhere in the audience, drunk and disorderly, was future Sex Pistols bassist Sid Vicious. The Ramones instantly became his favourite band, and Dee Dee his favourite Ramone.

"Sid loved The Ramones," says future Adam And The Ants guitarist Marco Pirroni, "though he hated their hair. Sid had great hair. They didn't. But he did get his ripped jeans and leather jacket look from The Ramones."

The Ramones' no-frills sound also had an instant impact on the nascent punk scene. When the Sex Pistols went into the recording studio with producer Chris Spedding, they brought in The Ramones' debut album and said, "This is what we want to sound like."

"The Ramones kick-started the whole UK punk thing."
CAPTAIN SENSIBLE

The Ramones, The Roundhouse, London, 1976

ELTON JOHN

MADISON SQUARE GARDEN, NEW YORK, AUGUST 1976

"Elton played 8 shows in little over a week and broke all the records for a rock act there. His popularity was just unparalleled. But I definitely saw two sides of Elton during his stay in New York. On stage, he was in great form. He'd be changing outfits, stomping around, playing the showman. Divine got up on stage with him. Billie Jean King, the tennis star, sang 'Philadelphia Freedom'. And his band rocked – especially Davey Johnstone and Ray Cooper. Elton just shook the place.

"Privately, I think it was a really tough time for him. *Rolling Stone* hired me to take pictures for a cover story, so I shot the live shows, but Elton was giving no interviews. Then the writer Cliff Jahr and I had this T-shirt made up that said 'Prisoner In New York' and arranged for it to be sent to him. I mean, Elton couldn't leave his hotel at that point. He'd only need to put his head out the window and people below would start screaming.

"It was a last-ditch attempt and it worked. We got a call next day saying, 'Come over at two o'clock.' He had the Elizabeth Taylor Suite at the Sherry Netherland Hotel, a fabulous suite: multiple bedrooms, dining room, kitchen, big, big living room. We assumed it would be full of people – managers, security, publicists, the whole entourage. But when we arrived, this houseboy answered the door and that was it. We had Elton to ourselves for three hours.

"The Elton we saw back at the hotel that day was completely different. He was dressed in sweat pants, and seemed a little tired. I didn't see ego at all. I found him rather reserved, sort of non-sexual. He was very much into his football team.

"Cliff was convinced that Elton was gay or at least bisexual. So we prearranged that when he started to ask questions on a football team or something, I would leave the room, which I did. Afterwards, Cliff said, 'I asked him all that stuff.' It was such a blockbuster of a story that *Rolling Stone* asked him to stretch it and ran it two issues in a row. It was a big deal. It was very rare for people to come out of the closet back then, especially someone at the height of his career." Ron Pownall, photographer

"It was rare for people to come out of the closet...especially at the height of their career."
RON POWNALL, PHOTOGRAPHER

Elton John, Madison Square Gardens, New York, 1976

THE PUNK ROCK FESTIVAL
100 CLUB, OXFORD STREET, LONDON, 20–21 SEPTEMBER 1976

Two nights of punk rock mayhem at London's 100 Club were marred when, on the second night, Sid Vicious threw a glass that struck a pillar and shattered, damaging a girl's eye in the process. The popular press seized on the incident, using it as a stick to beat the "evil" of rock's dangerous new cult. But the festival was also notable in giving rise to a band intent on taking the punk aesthetic to its extreme.

Siouxsie And The Banshees couldn't play. They didn't have a name. Or, until the eve of the show, any idea how to hold – let alone play – their instruments. But they weren't short of ideas. "One was to ruin a Beatles song like 'She Loves You'," says Siouxsie. "Then there was a plan to have a go at a Bay City Rollers or Donny Osmond song but I didn't know the words. Eventually, we settled for making a noise based around 'The Lord's Prayer'. At least I knew the words to that, and I wanted to do something beastly around

religion, trash a holy cow."

The Punk Rock Festival marked a significant turning-point, though some key players felt that in going overground, the movement was in danger of losing its essence. "The 100 Club Festival was massive," says Subway Sect's Rob Simmons, "with all these people queuing round the block to get in. But it was all over by then. Before then, [Johnny] Rotten would stick pins on a dinner jacket, or customise a T-shirt himself. As a stylist, he was fantastic. But at the 100 Club Festival, he was dressed in all [Westwood's] Sex clothes. The Pistols had become caught up in their own image."

"There were never big crowds before that," adds Subway Sect frontman Vic Godard. "And these were not punky people at all, but everyday people, tabloid readers. Most frightening for me was seeing this kid that lived down the bottom of my street in the queue. He didn't know I was even in a band."

FIRST NIGHT

SEX PISTOLS
THE CLASH
SIOUXSIE AND THE BANSHEES
SUBWAY SECT

SECOND NIGHT

CHRIS SPEDDING AND THE
VIBRATORS
THE BUZZCOCKS
THE DAMNED
STINKY TOYS

Opposite: Sex Pistols' Steve Jones, Johnny
Rotten and Glen Matlock.

Left: Johnny Rotten modelling Vivienne
Westwood's latest design, the bondage suit.
"Before then, Rotten was a fantastic stylist,"
says Subway Sect's Rob Simmons. "He'd
customize everything himself."

Left: Guitarist Marco Pirroni, a Banshee just for one night. Behind him are Siouxsie Sioux, Stephen Severin and, on drums, also making his stage debut, Sid Vicious.

Above, top: Sex Pistols' bassist Glen Matlock.

Above: The Damned's Dave Vanian and original guitarist, Brian James.

"Tonight, we're gonna do a one-hour set called Music From The Death Factory," said Throbbing Gristle frontman Genesis P-Orridge as the band prepared to assault all senses. "It's basically about the post-breakdown of civilization. You walk down the street and there's a lot of ruined factories and bits of old newspaper with stories about pornography and Page Three pin-ups blowing down the street. You turn a corner past the dead dog, and you see old dustbins. And over the ruined factory, there's a funny noise..."

Throbbing Gristle specialised in funny. And noises. And getting up everyone's noses. Unlike the younger punks, emerging around the same time, TG had a track record in public nuisance having grown out of performance art provocateurs COUM Transmissions. In fact, the ICA gig was ostensibly an add-on to a COUM retrospective exhibition, Prostitution, which – thanks to a few pornographic photographs and used tampons in Perspex cases – initially created far more headlines than the band's 'anti-music'.

"It's a sickening outrage!" complained Tory MP Nicholas Fairbairn. "Sadistic! Obscene! Evil!" His description of the perpetrators as "wreckers of civilization" was gleefully accepted by the group, who later used it in their publicity.

TG, which eclipsed COUM after Prostitution, were, P-Orridge maintained at the ICA, on a mission "to stop the decay of civilization through music". Many disputed this, citing the band's wilful cacophony of sinister sounds, created on customized instruments, tapes and electronics, as a black/bleak celebration of cultural collapse. The subject matter of the material aired at the ICA was hardly less palatable either. 'Very Friendly' recounted in gory detail one of the crimes committed by Ian Brady and Myra Hindley (alias The Moors Murderers). 'Zyklon B Zombie' was inspired by gas used in Nazi concentration camps. 'Slug Bait' was quite simply one of the most terrifying pieces of music ever performed.

But there was terrific irony – and a devastating social critique – in TG's work that, back in 1976, sounded remarkably fresh in a rock world that had become one-dimensional and self-satisfied. "It's nice to know there are so many pop fans in London," muttered P-Orridge as he surveyed the 600-strong ICA audience. The band wouldn't always play to such a large – or tolerant – crowd as the intriguing mix of punks, Hell's Angels and art critics who witnessed the emergence of the punk aesthetic in its rawest, most provocative state.

"Their, uh, music consisted of lots of weird sub-psychedelic taped sounds rolling around random keyboards played plonk-plonk style, lead guitar that Patti Smith would have been ashamed of and moronic bass on a superb Rickenbacker by old Genesis P-Orridge himself."
TONY PARSONS, *NEW MUSICAL EXPRESS*

PARLIAMENT

OAKLAND COLISEUM, SAN FRANCISCO, 21 JANUARY 1977

It was, claimed mainman George Clinton, one of the best live shows on the planet. Twenty musicians dressed in $10,000 worth of outlandish stage costumes: space-age clobber with huge wing collars, plenty of diamante flash – and a guitarist wearing a huge nappy. The undisputed star, though, was The Mothership, a flying saucer that descended onto the stage at the climax of each performance. As the band started up 'The Clones Of Dr Funkenstein', Clinton – alias Dr Funkenstein – would duly emerge resplendent in a white fur coat and sporting several pairs of shades.

Parliament's P-Funk Earth tour came hot on the heels of Parliament's *American Mothership* album, a gift for visual representation with its loose, though fashionable, storyline about aliens taking over the world. "It was," explained musical director Bernie Worrell to *Q* magazine's Toby Manning, "a movie, a Broadway play and some crazy science-fiction thing rolled into one."

Opposite: 'Dr Funkenstein', alias George Clinton, with nappy-wearing guitarist Gary Snider.
Below: The mothership descends on the Oakland Coliseum.
Overleaf: Parliament's extravagant bassist Bootsy Collins.

"I wanted to do something on a par with Kiss or Bowie and put a black spin on it."

GEORGE CLINTON

Parliament, Oakland Coliseum, San Francisco, 1977

ABBA

"It's the concert of the decade!" yelled the announcer repeatedly, as 25,000 people holding 25,000 umbrellas cheered and sang, in a vain hope that the rain might pass. It didn't, but then, no one seemed to mind as they waited the four hours between walking through the gates and the start of the show. "When we ran on to the stage it seemed the ovation would never end," remembered Agnetha Fältskog in her 1997 autobiography.

Adverse weather had threatened to jeopardize ABBA's eagerly anticipated Australian debut concert. The group were unable to rehearse their new string section properly, the outdoor arena was a quagmire even before the crowds began to arrive and, by the time the quartet took to the stage, there was a very real threat of electrocution ("We were terrified," Björn later admitted). A team of stagehands was hastily assembled to mop water away from the stage between songs. Even this failed to prevent Anni-Frid from slipping over and damaging her hip and two fingers during 'Waterloo'.

The sound, too, suffered as rain battered the banks of speakers either side of the stage, but with ABBAmania at fever pitch – "THEY'RE HERE!" announced the *Daily Mirror* when the group flew in four days earlier – not even the heavens were about to spoil the greatest pop party held Down Under since the days of Beatlemania. It was, the group later said of their 11-show Australian stint, the most dramatic two weeks of their career.

Dressed in their post-glam rock satins, with a hint of sportswear thrown in, the Swedish pop deities defied the gods and performed their *de rigueur* repertoire of hits, choice album tracks and carefully scripted between-songs banter with typically immaculate showbiz discipline. Near the climax of the set, their self-styled mini-musical 'The Girl With The Golden Hair' was performed without a hitch. A brief snatch of 'Waltzing Matilda',

played by Benny on accordion, was added to provide a little local colour. Miraculously, just one song, 'So Long', was sacrificed to the weather.

"We have probably never received such a rapturous reception anywhere," Agnetha concluded. The hysterical scenes that accompanied ABBA's first night in Sydney followed them throughout the tour, as they wound their way towards Perth, before flying home to Stockholm later in the month. It all provided a suitably stirring backdrop to *ABBA The Movie*, of course.

Overleaf, left: Agnetha Fältskog, who later recalled that ABBA's Australian tour was the "most incredible" of all her experiences with the band.
Right: Björn, Agnetha and Anni-Frid brave the adverse weather conditions with their customary good humour.

"The Australian tour was the most incredible of all the things that I experienced with ABBA."
AGNETHA FÄLTSKOG

ABBA, Sydney Showground, 1977   197

SEX PISTOLS
RANDY'S RODEO, SAN ANTONIO, TEXAS, 8 JANUARY 1978

"The Pistols could have come to New York and Los Angeles and the crowds would have kissed their asses. But [manager] Malcolm McLaren booked them into places like Memphis and Baton Rouge where people wanted to kill them. Especially in San Antonio.

"Randy's Rodeo was a bizarre meeting of Texas cowboys and punk rock, which wasn't remotely established in the United States at that point. The majority had come to see a freak show. It was a big place, like an old roller-skating rink, and some people

were wearing those safety pins through their noses that don't actually pierce the skin. There was a lot of aggression towards the Sex Pistols.

"As soon as the band got on stage, they began taunting the audience, saying things like, 'You cowboys are all faggots.' Sid Vicious used that old Iggy [Pop] line: 'You're the idiots who've paid your ten dollars. We're getting the last laugh.' The crowd responded by throwing millions of beer cans and whatever else at the stage. It was a really intense confrontation, and I knew

right away that I wasn't going up front to take my shots.

"Eventually, some punter down the front was really egging Sid on, so Sid just took his bass off and hit him with it. He was already a mess at that point, really fucked up and self-destructive in a way that nobody else in the band was even close to. Sid pushed the confrontation that McLaren wanted, blurring the border between art and life. I remember him telling me, 'I wanna be dead like Iggy before I'm 30.' But I said, 'Iggy's 35 and still alive!' He was a mess and really

"Oh, dear. Sidney's bass seems to have fallen off."
Johnny Rotten

unhappy on that tour.

"When the bass player takes his guitar off and hits somebody in the audience over the head, you know that things have got out of hand, that real danger is in the air. In New York, we had The Ramones who were obviously punk rock, but there was never this kind of confrontation. Their audience were fans. But these people who'd come to see the Pistols weren't. They just wanted to hate them."

Roberta Bayley, photographer

ROCK AGAINST RACISM
VICTORIA PARK, HACKNEY, LONDON, 30 APRIL 1978

"The song that epitomized the altruism of the event was 'Glad To Be Gay', by headliners The Tom Robinson Band, even though it had nothing to do with racism. It might as well have been 'Sing if you're glad to be black'. The message was that no matter who you are, you should have the freedom to be yourself.

"I was a teenage art student, living in Buckinghamshire, who dressed out of Oxfam. I was wearing plimsolls that I'd painted myself; one luminous green with red laces, the other bright red with green laces. I was a big X-Ray Spex fan and I loved Poly Styrene's whole aesthetic. She always seemed to be wearing home-made clothes which was quite different to the whole safety-pin, uniform of punk thing. I thought the whole point of punk was DIY: make your own clothes, make your own music, make your own art.

"I joined the march at Trafalgar Square and it took ages to get from central London to Victoria Park. There were police everywhere, all the way from start to finish, and everyone was chanting and waving a sea of placards. I was definitely anti-racist and into the politics of it, and understood the event as this big 'We're all in this together' thing. But when I put a pound in the bucket, I did so with some reluctance, because I wondered whether it was a rip-off. How do I know this pound is going anywhere!

"Steel Pulse were the main reggae band, and I'd been buying their singles, but I was really into The Clash. I'd seen them several times, but this wasn't their best gig by a long way. I'd never seen Sham 69 and when Jimmy Pursey came on stage with this stripy French

T-shirt, I thought he looked fantastic. Later on my mates told me that Sham 69's own gigs were quite different, very aggressive.

"My most vivid memory, though, is dancing to 'Glad To Be Gay'. I was with my mates, all quite macho bikers who rode Eastern European or old English machines, and who were really into the whole punk thing. I remember thinking, I'm not gay, so why am I singing and dancing to this? And what will all these guys think of me going berserk and making a hole in the mud?

"Victoria Park marked the end of punk for me. Punk had been about small gigs in sweaty clubs, filled with spit and gyrating bodies. There was this huge sexual thing going on in amongst all the camaraderie and pogoing. I never really listened to bands. I just went ballistic. And, despite its importance in the scheme of things, I couldn't do that at Victoria Park. You couldn't get close enough and it wasn't loud enough."

Simon Klein, marcher

Above, left: Oxfam chic legend X-Ray Spex's Poly Styrene.
Above: The Clash, punk rock's answer to The Rolling Stones.

Opposite, left: Clash bassist Paul Simonon.
Opposite, right: Sham 69's Jimmy Pursey (right) joined The Clash in stage. Sham 69's own gigs were often a magnet for violence.

THE GRATEFUL DEAD
SPHINX THEATRE, GIZA, EGYPT, 14–16 SEPTEMBER 1978

The idea of "The Trip" was intrinsic to everything The Grateful Dead stood for. Their music meandered magnificently, as if holding a mirror to the LSD experience. Their way of life seemed dedicated to transforming reality. Inevitably, the band's unquenchable quest for the esoteric crossed paths with the lure of ancient wisdom, and never more so than on the last night of their three-gig Egyptian sojourn when they performed in front of the Sphinx, with the Great Pyramid just behind, and a total eclipse of the moon taking place in the skies above.

After a rollercoaster of astonishing musical adventures that lasted from the mid-Sixties to the early Seventies, The Grateful

Dead appeared to run out of steam. Then in 1975, the Middle Eastern-influenced *Blues For Allah* brought some much-needed mystery and imagination back to their work. Suitably re-energized, they packed off bassist Phil Lesh early in 1978 to meet the Egyptian minister of culture. By March, everything was in place: The Grateful Dead's summer trip to Egypt, where they were to perform in the crucible of ancient civilization, was on.

For a band that rarely ventured beyond the borders of the United States, the venture was a huge undertaking. A plane was chartered, and the band and its entourage were joined by a number of fans ('Deadheads') who had forked out $999 apiece for the trip, which

"No cops, no parents!" beamed Jerry Garcia, the band's guitarist and spiritual leader.

included 12 nights in a hotel close to the pyramids. At 2.30pm on 5 September 1978, the long-haul post-psychedelic community touched down and walked right into a Cairo heatwave. Three days later, four trucks' worth of equipment duly followed.

By this time, the band and its extended family had settled into the colonial-style Mena House hotel – and the local lifestyle. Huge slabs of hashish were procured, stoner accoutrements were purchased at the markets, and a Grateful Dead flag was duly planted at the top of the Great Pyramid. Quizzical onlookers were bemused by the presence of the "moustached Californians".

The performances over the three nights couldn't hope to match those of the band's Haight-Ashbury heyday. The musicians weren't all in great shape – drummer Bill Kreutzmann had a broken wrist, Phil Lesh had been overdoing it, Keith Godchaux's keyboard was out of tune – and there had been unforeseen perils, such as the bats and bugs attracted by the stage lights. However, the "sound and light spectacle" promised on the tickets to the several hundred bliss-seekers who'd gathered each night was infinitely more than the sum of its parts. Even the notoriously static Bill Graham, San Francisco's leading concert promoter, was moved to admit: "One of the great experiences of my life was dancing to 'Sugar Magnolia' in front of the Great Pyramid."

The Grateful Dead, Sphinx Theatre, Egypt, 1978

SIOUXSIE AND THE BANSHEES/NICO

TOP RANK, CARDIFF, 15 OCTOBER 1978

Not every band inspired by the Sex Pistols wanted to sound like them, least of all Siouxsie And The Banshees, veterans of the 1976 Punk Rock Festival, who by autumn 1978 had eclipsed their contemporaries to become the most thrilling and uncompromising band around. To hardcore punks, they epitomized "no sell-out" belligerence. Their intelligence and angular, austere sound made them cheerleaders for the new, post-punk *avant-garde*. Even pop fans had hit on them, thanks to the recent success of their debut single 'Hong Kong Garden'. "There didn't seem to be any half measures with them," says The Human League's Phil Oakey, an early convert.

"Although The Slits were running them a close second, I knew that the Banshees were the greatest band in the world. Punk had been brilliant, galvanizing youth culture in a way not seen since the hippie explosion, which had all happened too early for my generation. What's more, it seemed to tap into a lineage that exonerated my idiosyncratic passion for the Velvet Underground, and more specifically Nico, whose intermittent solo career had produced four albums that sounded like nothing else.

"When Nico, who appeared to be at least as forbidding as her music, was revealed as the 'special guest' on the Banshees' first major UK tour, it made perfect sense to this 19-year-old. I had little doubt that when the tour rolled into Cardiff, where I was studying at the time, I'd be witnessing something I'd not forget. Well, I wasn't to be disappointed…

"I'd heard Nico booed before – in 1974, when I took a copy of *The Marble Index* along to the school music club. But the reception she received here was something else. Within seconds of walking on stage, her deep, Germanic bellow and droning harmonium were being cruelly mimicked by the impatient crowd. Three or four songs in and the hail of beer cans, cigarette butts and chewing gum (which had to be cut from her hair while she played) made a retreat inevitable. Even Siouxsie coming out to placate the crowd made little difference. It was a rude awakening that, despite punk's revolutionary rhetoric, the forces of reaction were rarely far away.

"Minutes later, I found myself backstage among a small group of shocked, sympathetic well-wishers. Nico barely spoke. A security guard said he'd watched her shoot up before the gig. But wearing a girlish smile as she gazed quietly into a mirror, Nico signed autographs and posed for photos. A transvestite from Swansea insisted we'd all have copies, but I never saw him/her again.

"Siouxsie And The Banshees, of course, saved the night."

Mark Paytress, audience member

Left: "If I had my gun I would shoot you all," deadpanned Nico, as she was forced off-stage by an audience oblivious to the debt the Banshees owed to the one-time Velvet Underground chanteuse.

Opposite: Touring their debut album, *The Scream*, in autumn 1978, Siouxsie And The Banshees were the most innovative and potentially revolutionary (anti-) rock band in the world.

"I ended up on stage shooting Steven Morris through the drum kit and Ian Curtis from behind looking out at the audience. That's when Peter Hook told me to f**k off."

MARTIN O'NEILL, PHOTOGRAPHER

"The local youth club organized a month-long series of weekly gigs, featuring four bands – The Freshies, Fast Cars, Joy Division and V2. It was a strange place to play because it was a mile and a half from Altrincham town centre and there were more obvious venues to play. I'd just started as a photographer on the *Sale And Altrincham Messenger* newspaper, so I'd turn up each week and take pictures, then go home and develop them. I'd go to the editor the following morning but he'd just put down his pipe and tell me to go away. They never got used.

"I took a lot more shots of Joy Division than I did of the other bands, so even at this stage in their career, there must have been something different about them. I started off in the middle of the crowd looking at the whole band. Then I got a lot closer to Ian Curtis. I ended up on stage shooting Steven Morris through the drum kit and Ian Curtis from behind looking out at the audience. That's when Peter Hook told me to fuck off. I hadn't arranged anything with the group beforehand, but apart from that they didn't seem to mind.

"I was quite excited as the band started, but as soon as Ian Curtis began to dance in that strange way, it scared the hell out of me. I thought, What's wrong with him? There's one shot where he looks straight at the camera, but other than that he's off in his own world. Perhaps it was the medication. He certainly wasn't self-conscious about his movements. He seemed to move without any connection to the music a lot of the time. He was certainly different. The first thing people say when they look at the photographs is, 'My god, look at the wallpaper. It's so '70s!' Then they say, 'Isn't the audience young.' A lot of the kids were just stood at the front with their arms folded. There didn't seem to be any dancing or pogoing. The kids look totally nonplussed. Though at the end of each song, there was a lot of clapping and cheering, so clearly a lot of people were already getting it."

Martin O'Neill, photographer

Joy Division, Bowdon Vale Youth Club, Manchester 1979

BOB MARLEY AND THE WAILERS

SUMMER GARDEN PARTY, CRYSTAL PALACE, LONDON, 7 JUNE 1980

Across an artificial pond, on a warm summer's day, Marley played his last ever concert in London. It had been the first city outside Jamaica to embrace him so warmly, notably at his legendary Lyceum shows back in July 1975. As he walked out on stage to the sound of 'Sun Is Shining' the intermittent rain that had threatened to blight the day ceased, and Bob Marley And The Wailers played out their set – promoting their latest *Uprising* album – in blissful sunshine. Less than a year after the open-air festival, on 11 May 1981, the man once described as "the Mick Jagger of reggae", but who is probably better remembered for bringing rebel music to a truly international audience, was dead.

"All I ever had is songs of freedom"
BOB MARLEY, 'REDEMPTION SONG'

Bob Marley And The Wailers, Crystal Palace, London, 1980 211

PUBLIC IMAGE LTD

THE RITZ, NEW YORK, 15 MAY 1981

"Ladies and gentlemen, here's Public Image Limited!" announced journalist Lisa Yapp, who had been involuntarily thrust onto the stage. The audience had been waiting for over an hour, and their chants of "PiL! PiL! PiL!" had grown ever more impatient. However, there was no sign of PiL, just a 40-foot video wall showing pre-recorded footage, mixed in with live video images of the trio – frontman John Lydon, guitarist Keith Levene and non-musical member Jeanette Lee – tinkering behind the screen.

For the first ten minutes or so, the audience was transfixed. It was, after all, a novel way to start a show. Besides, John Lydon was one-time Sex Pistol Johnny Rotten, and they had come to expect such diverting antics from a man now at the helm of post-punk's most artful combo. Perhaps they should have heeded Levene's on-screen words at the start of the event: "Rock and roll is dead. This is a new age of performance." For PiL had no intention of coming out from behind the screen – and the more the audience yelled, the more bottles and cans that were hurled at the screen, the more resolute the self-styled mixed media "company" became.

"You're not throwing enough," taunted Lydon at one point, taking a break during PiL's "set" of percussive bursts, feedback-drenched guitar and his own mock-Eastern yodelling. So they duly obliged. Shortly after Levene yelled an angry "If you destroy that screen, we will destroy you," the furious crowd began to dismantle the stage. After 25 minutes of "no-show", PiL retreated from behind the video screen to relative safety backstage, smiling all the way.

Left: John Lydon backstage with Ramones' bassist Dee Dee Ramone.

Opposite, top: Lydon, PiL's "media guru" Jeanette Lee and guitarist Keith Levene share a joke at the audience's expense.

Opposite, bottom: Fans search in vain for the invisible band.

Public Image Ltd., The Ritz, New York, 1981   213

Public Image Ltd, The Ritz, New York, 1981

"Silly f**king audience. Silly f**king audience."
John Lydon

Opposite: The audience grows increasingly impatient at PiL's infamous no-show at the Ritz in New York. The city's rare opportunity to see an ex-Pistol ended with the crowd pulling down a huge video screen behind which PiL had been hiding.

WOMAD Festival
SHEPTON MALLET, SOMERSET, 16–18 JULY 1982

While ostensibly white and working class, punk and its aftershocks did much to lift the lid on multicultural Britain, thanks in large part to affiliated organizations such as Rock Against Racism and The Anti-Nazi League. The crossover with reggae, largely down to Roxy Club DJ Don Letts and the broadmindedness of key players such as John Lydon, was only the most visible sign of a flourishing cultural eclecticism. Cabaret Voltaire, David Byrne and Eno began to utilize non-western sound sources, while The Slits and The Pop Group were increasingly drawn to African rhythms.

It wasn't just the new iconoclasts who sought to displace, or perhaps enrich, the rock tradition by searching elsewhere for new sounds. Peter Gabriel, one-time Genesis frontman and one of a small handful of musicians who survived the new wave with reputation intact, hatched the idea for a truly international music festival in 1980. By summer 1982, his vision was realized. Dozens of acts, from all parts of the globe, transformed the Royal Bath and West Showground at Shepton Mallet in England's West Country into a multicultural – and multicoloured – village. From Indonesian gamelan to Japanese koto music, tribal rhythms from deepest Africa to ska beats from urban London, Gabriel's World of Music Arts And Dance festival was a triumph in every way – except financially. That was largely down to a national rail strike that meant no more than 20,000 made it to the West Country. (Gabriel was obliged to reform Genesis for a WOMAD benefit show later that year.)

In order to pull in the numbers, various big-name rock acts had been roped in, including Echo And The Bunnymen, Simple Minds, The Beat and Gabriel himself, but it was the more unfamiliar names that stole the show. The magical sound of a large gamelan orchestra from Indonesia filled the air one afternoon. More dramatic still were the pounding beats and chants of The Burundi Drummers, who proved so popular that extra performances had to be hastily scheduled.

Of the domestic contingent, it was cult Industrial Music band 23 Skidoo who made the most notable contribution. Opening on one of the main stages at midday, shaven headed and with their faces camouflaged, they unleashed an astonishing collage of electronic sound, tape loops and chillingly blown Tibetan thigh bones, a blast from the heart of England's post-industrial wastelands. It seemed far more in keeping with the weekend than the contributions of the conventional rock crowd-pullers.

A WORLD OF MUSIC ARTS & DANCE

A HANDBOOK GUIDE TO THE W.O.M.A.D. FESTIVAL THE ROYAL BATH AND WEST SHOWGROUND 16–18 JULY 1982

Centre Ocean Stream

WOMAD Festival, Shepton Mallet, Somerset, 1982

Previous page, left: The Drummers of Burundi leave the stage after another astonishing display of syncopated rhythms from Central Africa. Although several 'Western' acts performed at the inaugural WOMAD festival, it was the musical riches from Asia and Africa that made the more lasting impression on the 20, 000 people who managed to make it to the festival despite a national rail strike.

Opposite: Echo And The Bunnymen's Ian McCullough bringing some monochrome, post-punk normality to the most exotic music festival of all time.

Left: The Drummers of Burundi and Echo And The Bunnymen join forces.

WOMAD Festival, Shepton Mallet, Somerset, 1982   219

Grand
Gestures

AFTER A VIRTUALLY UNINTERRUPTED 30-YEAR STRETCH, THAT HAD SEEN THE ORIGINAL ROCK'N'ROLLERS ECLIPSED BY A SERIES OF EVER MORE ESOTERIC SUBCULTURAL GROUPS, THE '80S DELIVERED ROCK AND POP BACK INTO THE HANDS OF THE MAINSTREAM. PERHAPS IT WAS THE INEVITABLE CONSEQUENCE OF LATE CAPITALISM, WHICH DEMANDED THAT EVERYTHING BE UNDERTAKEN ON A GRAND SCALE. MORE PROSAICALLY, IT WAS JUST AS LIKELY TO HAVE BEEN A REACTION TO PUNK'S CORNERSHOP AESTHETIC, WHICH WOULD SOONER SPIT UPON THE SOCIETY OF THE SPECTACLE THAN BECOME PART OF IT.

IT WAS THE ERA WHEN STADIUM ROCK BECAME THE NORM, RATHER THAN THE EXCEPTION. WHEN TECHNOLOGY BEGAN TO DICTATE TO MUSICIANS, NOT VICE VERSA. WHEN THE TRIUMPH OF STYLE, OF CONSPICUOUS CONSUMPTION ARTFULLY PROPOSED BY DAVID BOWIE DURING TH '70S, WAS MORE OBVIOUSLY HARNESSED TO CHASING THE DOLLAR THAN SATISFYING A CREATIVE IMPATIENCE.

IF THE PREVAILING SOUND HAD BECOME THAT OF THE SWIPED CREDIT CARD, THERE WERE NOTABLE POCKETS OF RESISTANCE. THE PUNK-PROMPTED INDEPENDENT SECTOR HAD DROPPED THE REVOLUTIONARY RHETORIC AND BEEN GIVEN A NEATER, 'INDIE' MAKEOVER, BUT IT STILL CARRIED SIGNIFICANT SUBCULTURAL WEIGHT, EVEN IF IT INCREASINGLY RELIED ON THE BUILDING BLOCKS OF ROCK'S GLORIOUS PAST IN ORDER TO CREATE ITS OWN, FAME-DRIVEN FUTURE. FOR INNOVATION, THOUGH, MUCH OF THE REAL ACTIVITITY TOOK PLACE IN THE NEWLY INVIGORATED DANCE MUSIC FIELDS. PUBLIC ENEMY REVOLUTIONIZED BLACK MUSIC WITH THEIR INCENDIARY RAPS AND DISOBEDIENT BEATS. AND BACK IN EUROPE, THE CULT OF THE DJ WAS RESCUED FROM ITS LOWLY STATUS ONE MAGNIFICENT SUMMER IN IBIZA. EVENTUALLY, ROCK TOO WAS ROUSED FROM ITS SLUMBER WHEN IN 1991 NIRVANA EMERGED WITH AN INSTANTLY CLASSIC FUSION OF HARD ROCK AND PUNK.

WHEN THE BAND'S FRONTMAN KURT COBAIN KILLED HIMSELF, IN APRIL 1994, HE LEFT POPULAR MUSIC IN A CONSIDERABLY HEALTHIER STATE THAN IT WAS IN WHEN THE BAND BROKE BIG THREE YEARS EARLIER. IT WAS A HIGH PRICE TO PAY, BUT THESE HAD BEEN DESPERATE TIMES – AND COBAIN WAS A DESPERATE, IDEALIST MAN-MARTYR.

MICHAEL JACKSON

The Temptations, The Four Tops, Smokey Robinson – everyone was there to pull out all the stops for Motown's 25th anniversary show in southern California – but the night will always be remembered for one dramatic moment: it was the first time Michael Jackson unveiled his infamous "Moonwalk" dance.

Already an international superstar after some 15 years in the public eye, Jackson's fame had recently reached even greater levels with the release of *Thriller*, a multi-Grammy-winning album that ended up spending several months at the top of the US chart. As his brothers left the stage after a joint Jacksons routine, Michael launched into 'Billie Jean', which he punctuated with huge pelvic thrusts and what seemed like a vaguely sinister reverse walk, as if he was being operated by invisible strings. The routine brought an almost disbelieving audience to its feet. After it was broadcast on television two months later, it was obvious that the boy/man in the sparkling socks and tuxedo had just moonwalked his way into King of Pop infamy.

...but the night will always be remembered for one dramatic moment: it was the first time Michael Jackson unveiled his infamous "Moonwalk" dance.

QUEEN

ROCK IN RIO, RIO DE JANEIRO, BRAZIL, 12–19 JANUARY 1985

Each ticket boldly predicted "The Best Festival Of All Time". Well, it was certainly the biggest. Ninety hours of music, spread across ten days, with a combined audience of three million, the first and most memorable Rock In Rio exceeded even Brazilian businessman and organizer Roberto Medina's wildest expectations. That was thanks, in large part, to Queen, whose performances, including a climactic last night show, remain a turning point in rock's long, slow invasion of Latin America.

Frontman Freddie Mercury was the perfect star for the Eighties' obsession with gesture and flash, and his inimitably kinky kind of grandeur always worked best on the biggest stages imaginable. However, even he had his work cut out in Rio where, in front of 300,000 bronzed, beaming party animals, he walked onto a 21,000 square foot stage big enough to have held all the participating bands at once. As Freddie looked out towards the crowd, which greeted the band with deafening applause, he saw nothing but faces, flags and the most festive atmosphere he had ever

experience as a performer. Beyond the purpose-built arena was a virtual city with dozens of shops, including the world's largest McDonald's, and further still the mountains around Barra da Tijuca. It was an extraordinary setting and, typically, Freddie Mercury admirably rose to the occasion.

The set spanned the entire length of Queen's career, from their early Seventies nearly-hit 'Keep Yourself Alive' through to recent successes such as 'Hammer To Fall' and 'Radio Gaga', the latter accompanied by a sea of hands clapping in time. The only blip came when Mercury changed into his ladyboy outfit for 'I Want To Break Free', an act that upset a macho minority among the crowd. That didn't stop Freddie from falling in love with the place, though. "I'd like to buy up the entire continent and install myself as president," he told *Record Mirror*.

"The sunshine makes such a difference. People are allowed to flower here. They're a wonderful audience and I love their displays of emotion." FREDDIE MERCURY

THE JESUS AND MARY CHAIN

NORTH LONDON POLYTECHNIC, LONDON, 15 MARCH 1985

The post-punk dream of permanent musical revolution had faded. As the success of Postcard Records' Orange Juice and Rough Trade's The Smiths had proved, the three-minute pop song was back, albeit with a whiff of retro cool, and the meaning of independent music had changed forever.

Into what had now become an alternative pop space came The Jesus And Mary Chain: punkish name, rock'n'roll attitude, penchant for errant Pink Floyd man Syd Barrett and Heroin Thrills T-shirts. On record, they sounded like a textbook collision of The Velvet Underground and Phil Spector. The Mary Chain got busted for drugs and the critics loved them.

By March 1985, less than a year after they had moved down from East Kilbride in Scotland to London, The JAMC were poised for great things. Their second single, 'Never Understand', a classic slice of chainsaw-driven surf-pop, had just been released and they now had major label backing.

When the band walked off stage after 20 minutes and showed no signs of coming back, the crowd began to trash the equipment.

The queues outside North London Poly in 15 March told their own story. Hundreds of fans were unable to get into the already oversubscribed gig, despite the best efforts of two band members, who attempted to prise open the doors and let disgruntled punters in. The police came, and promptly left. Then someone from support band Meat Whiplash decided to throw a wine bottle into the crowd. He was set upon, and the band quietly retreated.

As if the night needed any more tension, the JAMC left it another hour before ambling on stage, which, as was customary, was virtually bare save for a couple of amps and a stand-up drum kit. After 20 minutes of pop feedback, they ambled off again. Feeling cheated, the audience yelled for more. When that didn't work, they began hurling beer cans at the stage. Still the Mary Chain failed to materialize. A stage invasion ensued, the band's equipment was trashed and the police were called out again. Eventually, the fighting stopped, but there was no more Jesus And Mary Chain that evening.

Alan McGee, the band's manager and Sex Pistols devotee, lapped it up. "Friday night proved that people are crying out for the first division excitement that The Jesus And Mary Chain provides," he declared. Claiming that "the audience were not smashing up the hall, they were smashing up pop music," McGee seized his moment and grandly concluded: "This is truly art as terrorism."

The Jesus And Mary Chain, North London Polytechnic, 1985

WHAM!
PEKING WORKER'S GYMNASIUM, CHINA 7 APRIL 1985

Selling a duo that seemed to epitomize the rampant individualism of Thatcher's Britain to communist China didn't come easy. In fact, it took Simon Napier-Bell, the band's colourful manager, two years and 13 trips before achieving his dream of making Wham! the first major Western pop act to perform in the workshop of the world.

Despite the ideological differences between London and Beijing, Wham!'s clean-cut image suited the authorities in the People's Republic. Ever vigilant in matters of youthful dissent, they'd been fairly keen to keep the wilder excesses of rock and pop from its borders, and Napier-Bell didn't have to tell too many fibs when he stressed that Wham! played "cheerful uncomplicated music [with] the absence of any hint of anarchy or teenage aggression". When it looked like Queen might be allowed in the country first, Wham!'s manager did his damnedest to portray the rock band as the epitome of Western depravity.

Despite little publicity (in China at least, for the breakthrough was hyped up throughout the West), all 15,000 seats in the keenly policed auditorium were occupied. As George Michael and Andrew Ridgeley bounced onto the stage, they sowed the seeds for a new era in east–west cultural relations. Napier-Bell was struck by the sense of culture shock, recalling how the audience barely understood the most basic cues – clapping in the wrong places, not knowing what to do when songs finished. By the end of the show, though, the place had come alive, with youngsters out of their seats and dancing.

One month later, when Napier-Bell was back in the country, he'd learned about another, more recent happening in the stadium. This time, again in front of a huge crowd, there had been a show trial. Several petty criminals had been sentenced to death, taken away and shot in the back of the head in a nearby field – but presumably not with the sound of Wham!'s 'Freedom' still ringing in their ears.

LIVE AID

ONE 16-HOUR CONCERT

TWO VENUES

69 ACTS

GLOBAL AUDIENCE: 1.5 BILLION PEOPLE

OPENING SONG: STATUS QUO'S 'ROCKING ALL OVER THE WORLD'

CLOSING SONG: 'WE ARE THE WORLD'

TARGET FIGURE: £1 MILLION

FUNDS PLEDGED TO RELIEVE THE FAMINE IN AFRICA: $140 MILLION

LIVES SAVED: BETWEEN ONE AND TWO MILLION

COMMONLY KNOWN AS: "THE GREATEST SHOW ON EARTH"

"Give us your f**king money now, please!"
LIVE AID ORGANIZER, BOB GELDOF

Live Aid, Wembley Stadium, London and JFK Stadium, Philadelphia, 1985

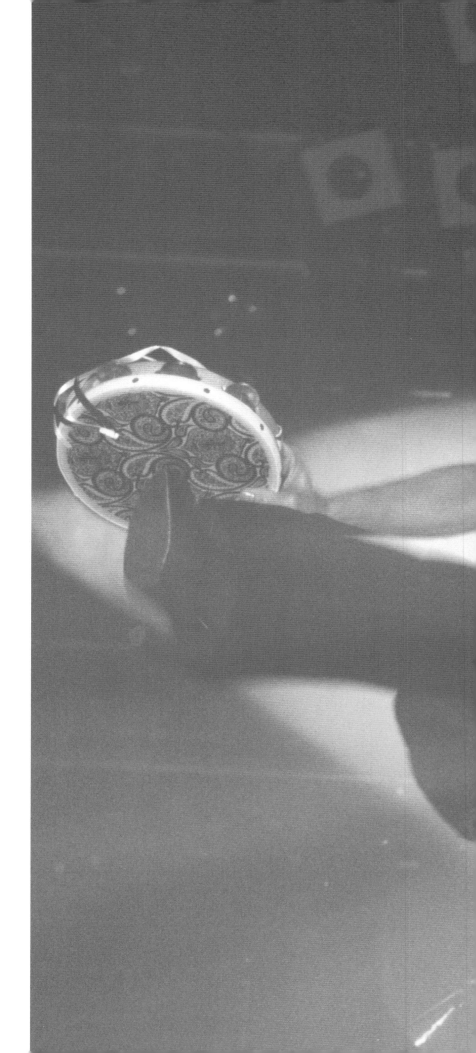

PRINCE
WEMBLEY ARENA, LONDON, 12–14 AUGUST 1986

Part Jimi Hendrix, part James Brown and part a one-man Sly And The Family Stone, Prince gave an impish twist to music old and contemporary, creating a sound – and a look – that virtually defined the 1980s.

These historic Wembley shows, which kicked off a 15-date European tour in support of his *Parade* album, were significantly less theatrical than Prince's previous visits. Instead of the expected on-stage spectacular, Prince now chose to rely on his own hyper-active persona and extraordinary musical dexterity – though he couldn't resist nipping off for a few costume changes. On the final Wembley date, he even shared the limelight with two home-grown heroes, inviting Sting and Rolling Stones guitarist Ron Wood to join him for a version of the Stones' 'Miss You'. Breathless and yet almost benevolent, this truly was a man at the peak of his powers.

"Prince is arguably the finest live rock act in the world today."
ANTHONY DeCURTIS, *ROLLING STONE*

Morrissey, pictured at the festival of the Tenth Summer, at Manchester's G-Mex, weeks before The Smiths' hometown swansong.

The Smiths, Free Trade Hall, Manchester, 1986

THE SMITHS

"When my brother was at university in Manchester, my mum used to put me on a National Express coach and I'd visit him, listening to The Smiths all the way there. One time, when I was 14, we were at his girlfriend's party when someone mentioned that The Smiths were playing. We headed straight for the venue, only to discover that all the tickets had gone. Eventually this lad sold us one for five pounds, which seemed cheap bearing in mind it was a sell-out. My brother, who'd seen them a few times, let me have it. We were both so thrilled I was going in, we forgot to make arrangements to meet after the show. He drove back to the party; I went to see The Smiths!

"I'd never been to a concert before so I was nervous and excited. I was miles away from home and a little frightened because everyone around me in this huge, seated hall was heavily northern. I was just this country girl from Andover, too scared even to get a drink from the bar. In fact I don't remember having any money.

"I knew from footage I'd seen on TV that The Smiths came on stage to an excerpt from [Prokofiev's] *Romeo And Juliet*. When that started up, things became quite surreal. It was hard feeling that emotional and not having a companion to share it all with. I knew all the songs. 'Vicar In A Tutu' was a fave. And 'Frankly, Mr Shankly', which my friend and I used to 'play' on badminton rackets when we should have been doing school sports. I screamed and sang along, especially when they played 'Meat Is Murder'. I'd turned vegetarian at 11.

"It was really all about Morrissey, I suppose. I was obsessed with him, ever since seeing him on *Pop Quiz* wearing a bright pink ladies' blouse with white spots on it. I never fancied him; I liked his sense of humour. Through him I got into Joe Orton, Kenneth Williams, various films and playwrights. Strange stuff for a 14-year-old, I suppose. Where I lived, nobody was into that stuff – or The Smiths – at all. Now I was surrounded by people who felt the same as me.

"After they'd finished with 'Bigmouth Strikes Again', I heard someone shouting my name, looked round and saw my brother clambering across the seats towards me. 'Keep shouting,' he said, 'and I'll get a free encore.' No luck. Though we didn't know it, The Smiths would only play one more UK show after this homecoming gig. But for me, this is the one. I lived off it for weeks. Still do, really..."

Donna, audience member

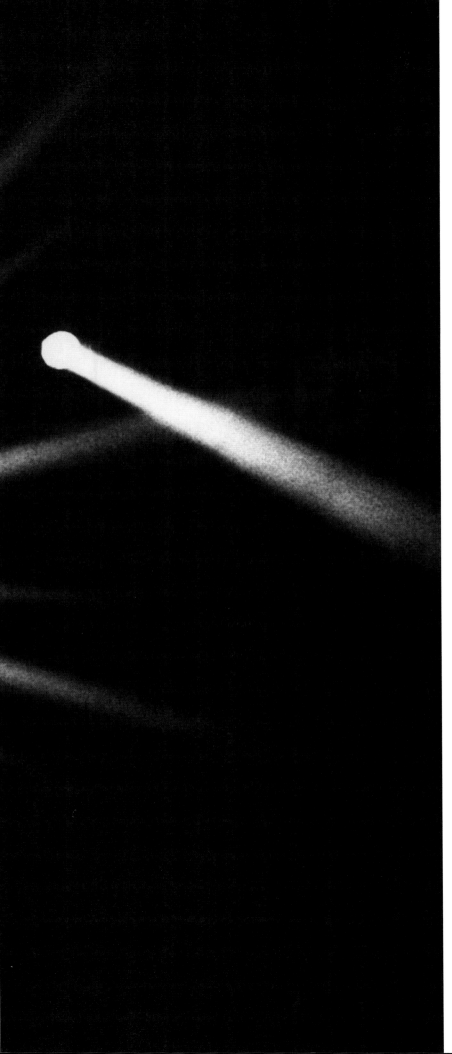

AMNESIA
IBIZA, 1987

The fastest beating heart of the second summer of love was found on Ibiza, one of a small group of Balearic islands off the eastern coast of Spain. That's where, in a small club called Amnesia, the Spanish house DJ Alfredo, enraptured a quartet of visiting DJs. Suitably inspired, Paul Oakenfold, Danny Rampling, Nicky Holloway and Trevor Fung returned to Britain where they started their own club nights, spinning Alfredo-style mixes to a new E'd up generation. And clubbing was never the same again...

A new generation of pleasure seekers tripped the lights fantastic together with a new generation of DJs, pulsating house music and the new acid-lite wonder drug, ecstasy.

Amnesia, Ibiza, 1987   237

Public Enemy, Montreux Rock Festival, Montreux, Switzerland, 1988

PUBLIC ENEMY
MONTREUX ROCK FESTIVAL, MONTREUX, SWITZERLAND, 1988

The air was thick with the sound of police sirens. The stage was filled with uniformed men in military fatigues, static and intimidating, hiding behind dark glasses, and wielding fake Uzis. Around them were a handful of musicians. Terminator X scratched, Flavor Flav bounced manically, an outsize clock swaying surreally from his neck, and mainman Chuck D – a magnificent hybrid of Malcolm X and Clark Gable – delivered some of the most incendiary, revolutionary rhymes ever heard in popular music.

There was no doubt who was on stage, and the name said it all. Public Enemy: the most important band of the decade, and one of the most significant in a century of popular music. In raising black consciousness, this band from Queens, New York, raised the knowledge bar of everyone else as well. In changing the rules of the recording process, Public Enemy transformed the landscape of contemporary culture. Do believe the hype.

"Too black...too strong."
BRING THE NOISE, PUBLIC ENEMY

Public Enemy's dynamic duo, Chuck D and Flavor Flav.

The blonde ponytail may have been fake, but there was nothing remotely fraudulent about Madonna's ambition, which by 1990 had taken her to the peak of pop superstardom. Cue the *Blonde Ambition* tour, part pop show, part Broadway extravaganza, that visited 27 cities in four months, creating headlines – and a few controversies – wherever it went.

Having rocketed to fame in 1984, and revealing the depth of her ambition the following year with her first tour, a devastatingly upbeat appearance at Live Aid and her first major film appearance (*Desperately Seeking Susan*), Madonna truly came of age in 1989 with the *Like A Prayer* album. That same year, she commissioned flamboyant designer Jean-Paul Gaultier to work on costumes for her third major tour. With the star sketching out rough designs, the pair emerged with a series of costumes that drew inspiration from Weimar Berlin and New York gay bars, Helmut Newton-style fetishism and the austerity of the flamenco dancer.

Madonna's capacity for creative change and pop spectacle echoed that of David Bowie more than a decade earlier. By the time of the *Blonde Ambition* tour, though, everything could be done on a far grander scale – and it was. The show unfolded from a factory setting to a Middle Eastern-style boudoir, before a church-like scene, complete with huge pillars and chandeliers, gave way to a finale of Broadway-style cheesiness. However, in her kinky conical bras, girdles and fishnets, Madonna made sure that the grand theatrics, and the troupe of dancers who constantly surrounded her, never deflected attention away from the star attraction.

The explosion of female sexuality that had always been at the heart of Madonna's appeal prompted calls for the show to be banned both in Toronto and in Rome, where the Vatican took particular offence at the prospect of the masturbation sequence during 'Like A Virgin'. Although the threatened arrest failed to materialize in Canada, papal power in Italy was strong enough to produce the only empty seats during the entire tour. However, the media-savvy Material Girl knew only too well that the acres of newsprint that inevitably followed would provide more than adequate compensation.

"Being blonde is definitely a different state of mind ... It has some incredible sort of sexual connotations.
Men really respond to it."
MADONNA

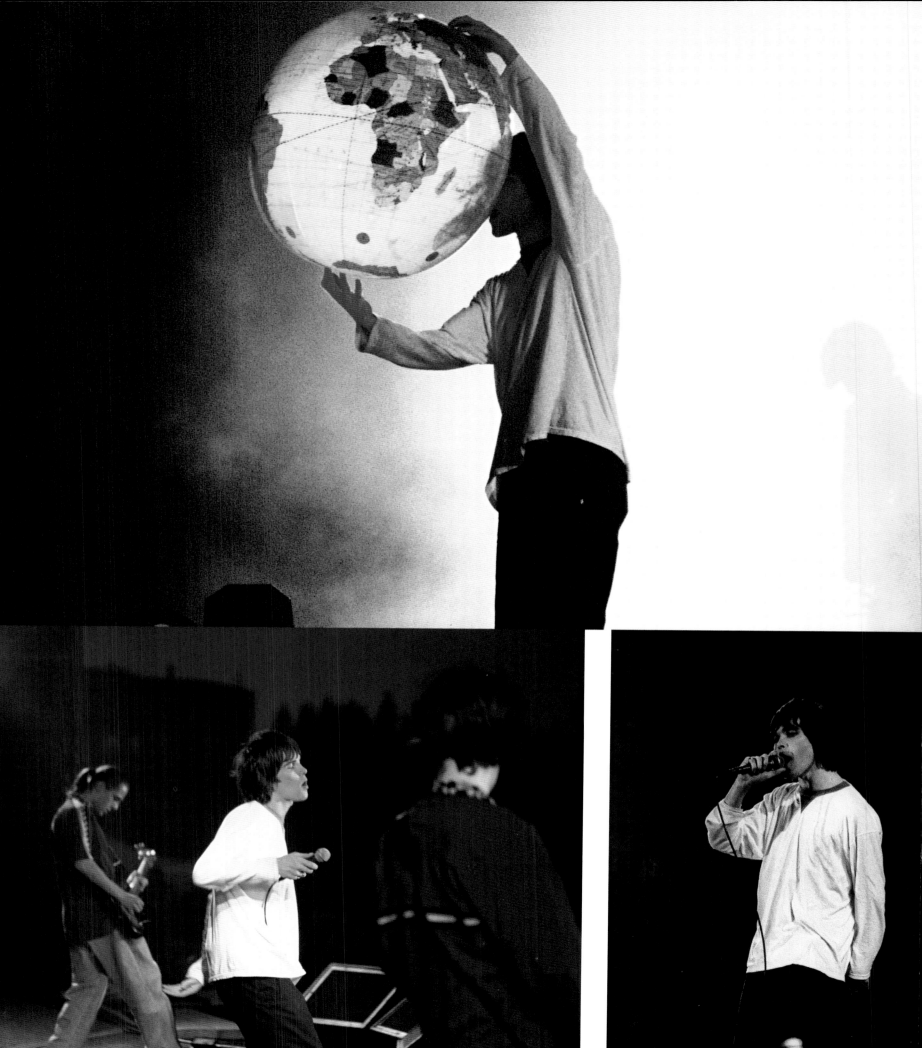

THE STONE ROSES

"Spike Island was where the '90s started. The Roses provided the dream and set the template for every British guitar band of the '90s." JOHN ROBB, JOURNALIST

It was the night kaleidoscopic pop met acid house, where flared trousers flapped and ultra-brite baggy shirts glowed in the dark under a carpet of bowl haircuts and Remi hats. The night when Stone Roses' frontman Ian Brown proudly declared, "Time! Time! Time! The time is now."

That's how it felt to a generation that had been desperately seeking their own indie guitar heroes, lads who were also plugged in to ecstasy culture and were unafraid to dance. It was no surprise that a band from Manchester fitted the bill, nor that this rum site on a peninsula facing the River Mersey near Widnes provided the venue for the event of 1990. "It was a bit depressing to find yourself in a horrible field surrounded by huge electric pylons, factories and chemical plants," St Etienne's Bob Stanley told *Q* magazine several years later.

Noel Gallagher, then a roadie for another Manchester band of bowl-heads The Inspiral Carpets, regarded Spike Island as "a cultural watershed – great bands, great setting, great vibe," he said, adding that the day was let down only by a "shit sound". In truth, the warm-up DJs – including Gary Clail's On-U Sound System, Paul Oakenfold and Frankie Knuckles – didn't work either, failing to generate much enthusiasm among the audience who preferred to sit around and get stoned. Even The Stone Roses' performance was hardly among their best, only really igniting towards the end of the set, when guitarist John Squire freed himself up with some blistering, Hendrix-inspired workouts. But sometimes the event, the moment itself is enough. The audience left with the floaty pop melodies of 'Elephant Stone', 'She Bangs The Drums' and the evocative 'I Wanna Be Adored' spinning round their heads, and the unshakeable belief that this had truly been An Event, the first of the new decade.

244   **REM, The Borderline, London, 1991**

REM
The Borderline, Orange Yard, London, 14–15 March 1991

It was, said REM's guitarist Peter Buck with a little added spice, "the worst reviewed show we ever did". One *Melody Maker* journalist aside, everyone else wedged into the tiny central London club over two nights in 1991 believed they had just witnessed the most relaxed shows ever performed in public by a major international rock band. REM were in town to celebrate the release of their latest album, *Out Of Time*, and had invited a handful of well-chosen guests – Peter Holsapple, Billy Bragg, Robyn Hitchcock – to join them for two distinctly low-key performances. Those who managed to squeeze into the tiny 275-capacity venue were treated to two three-hour sets, where songs such as Tim Hardin's 'Reason To Believe', Lee Hazlewood and Nancy Sinatra's 'Jackson' and The Byrds' 'You Ain't Goin' Nowhere' liberally punctuated REM material from all parts of their career. In keeping with the mood of the shows, everyone, even support act The Chickasaw Mud Puppies from REM's native Athens, Georgia, performed under a pseudonym.

Billy Bragg was Comrade, singer Michael Stipe The Reverend Bingo and, of course, REM took the best name of all: Bingo Hand Job.

Singer Michael Stipe, pictured around the time of the legendary Borderline show.

THE PIXIES

"It took The Pixies to put me back on the right track and off the whole macho punk rock trip."
KURT COBAIN

The band that opened the door for the early 1990s alternative rock phenomenon played their last major public gigs in Britain at the Brixton Academy. After a secret show at the Mean Fiddler in Willesden, North-West London, The Pixies joined U2 on tour in the States before calling it a day in 1992.

Thirteen years later, The Pixies chose the same Brixton venue to host a four-night residency during their Pixies' *Sell Out* comeback tour.

The Pixies' bassist, Kim Deal (right) and frontman, Black Francis (opposite).

LOLLAPALOOZA TOUR
LOCATIONS IN THE UNITED STATES, JULY–SEPTEMBER 1992

MAIN STAGE: RED HOT CHILI PEPPERS, MINISTRY, ICE CUBE, SOUNDGARDEN, THE JESUS AND MARY CHAIN, PEARL JAM, LUSH, TEMPLE OF THE DOG

SECOND STAGE: JIM ROSE TRAVELLING CIRCUS, SHARKBAIT, ARCHIE BELL, PORNO FOR PYROS, CYPRESS HILL, STONE TEMPLE PILOTS, RAGE AGAINST THE MACHINE

The brainchild of Jane's Addiction frontman Perry Farrell, Lollapalooza was a travelling rock festival that showcased what corporate America (dis)regarded as alternative rock. Launched in summer 1991, Farrell – now fronting Porno For Pyros, assembled an even bigger bill for '92. Among the small British contingent were Lush, whose Phil King and Chris Acland kept a tour diary:

San Francisco Shoreline Amphitheater, 19 July

"Second night of the tour. Weird scenes backstage. Lifto from the Jim Rose Travelling Circus is sitting eating breakfast, shaven-headed, wearing stockings, high heels and draped in a kimono. Later he will be seen hanging unfeasibly heavy weights from various parts of his anatomy..."

Seattle Kitsap Country Fairgrounds, 22 July

"Once Pearl Jam start playing we find that we have no choice but to evacuate our Portakabin dressing room. Literally everything in the room starts vibrating to the beat of the bass drum. What's it going to be like when Ice Cube's on?"

Left: Anthony Kiedis and a near-naked Flea.
Below left: Emma Anderson and flame-haired Miki Berenyi from Lush.
Below right: Eddie Vedder and Pearl Jam.

Cleveland Blossom Music Center, 29 July

"Anthony from the Chili Peppers was seen hobbling around on crutches today. He snapped his Achilles tendon last night after jumping in the air and landing on his microphone stand. The first of many casualties."

Boston Great Woods, 7 August

"During Ministry's set, huge clods of earth started to bounce on to the stage. In the distance, fires were lit which the audience were moshing around. Kinda tribal. Kinda Lollapalooza."

Dallas, 6 September

"It's come to the end of the tour and everything's getting a bit mad. Ministry destroyed their bus last night. Our guitar tech has broken his foot playing rock'n'roll basketball. Cath from T-shirts is on crutches after treading barefoot on broken glass trying to break up a top skinhead brawl. Fritzy from Ministry breaks his hand hitting someone. And Mike from Pearl Jam has fractured his foot. [Lush's] Miki dives off the stage during Ministry's set and there's no one to catch her. She's rushed to hospital on a stretcher in a neck brace."

Los Angeles Irvine Meadows, 13 September

"It's the last day of the tour and it's chaos backstage. The world and his wife are here. Someone staggers into our dressing room asking if he can use our potty. He is somewhat surprised to see Dave and Stone from Pearl Jam and Bill from Ministry dressed up as ladies. Everyone plays with everyone else today. It's beginning to look like a deranged Live Aid. Then...that's it. Regrets? We had a few. We never did get to see the Jim Rose Circus snort [Jesus And Mary Chain's] Jim Reid's diarrhoea. Still, you can't have everything..."

CASTLEMORTON RAVE
MALVERN HILLS, WORCESTERSHIRE, 21–24 MAY 1992

A cultural revolution of sorts occurred in 1988 when the mass popularity of a new drug, ecstasy, coincided with the emergence of a new era of dance music. More worrying still, at least for the authorities, was the trend for huge, out-of-town raves, unlicensed happenings that usually took place around the M25, the motorway that circled Greater London.

This dynamic take on the late Sixties free festival vibe reached a head over the May Bank Holiday weekend 1992, near a sleepy village at the foot of the Malvern Hills. The brainchild of dance collective Spiral Tribe, the country's biggest illegal rave attracted a swarm of sound systems and DJs, and up to 40,000 ravers and travellers.

Gloriously disorganized, Castlemorton was in reality a series of individual parties that rolled out across the countryside in a pulsing, technicolour splash. It was all too much for Middle England, whose newspapers conjured up a series of misleading headlines, such as the one that claimed "Hippies Fire Flares At Police". (As a show of defiance, a lit object was loosely directed at a police helicopter that circled aggressively above.)

After the police broke up the party, 14 people were subsequently charged with causing a public nuisance, though their cases were thrown out. The Conservative government finally exacted its revenge in 1994, when it passed the Criminal Justice Bill, which effectively prevented such scenes of mass joyous disorder from ever happening again.

"Everybody was off their faces."
ANONYMOUS RAVER

Just 18 months had passed since Nirvana signed their major label deal, and less than 12 since their second album *Nevermind* had taken the American rock market by surprise. But by August 1992, Nirvana, easily the biggest band in the world, at least in terms of influence and media coverage if not sales, were on the cusp of splitting, and frontman Kurt Cobain was dicing dangerously with death. At least, that's what the innuendo beneath the headlines suggested.

Throughout the day, the last in a rainy and mud-spattered weekend at Britain's longest-running rock festival, the crowd nervously awaited Nirvana's arrival. Even if they did make it, many half-expected some "This will be the last time" announcement from the stage, but it would be a long wait, because first there was a supporting cast that had been virtually handpicked by Cobain – on the basis of "no lame-ass limey bands", apparently in revenge for the British media's prying ways. From Nirvana's home patch in the Pacific North West came The Screaming Trees, Mudhoney and early scenemakers The Melvins. L7 chimed with Kurt's penchant for all-women bands, Björn Again with the band's fondness for ABBA on the tour coach. Nick Cave and Pavement pulled in the numbers, while Eugenius were a spin-off of Cobain indie faves The Vaselines.

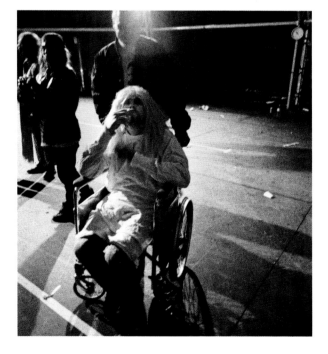

None of this really mattered, though, because Reading 1992 was all about Nirvana. The band had already visited Australia, Japan and continental Europe earlier that year, and in recent weeks all the attention had focused on Cobain, his wife Courtney Love and their new baby, Frances Bean, born 12 days before the gig. Not all of the doom-mongering was misplaced. Kurt and Courtney had suffered so much abuse in the press that they were faced with an instant custody battle for their child, a situation prompted by a story in *Vanity Fair* that spoke openly of the couple's drug use. One wildly inaccurate headline claimed, "ROCK STAR'S BABY BORN A JUNKIE". Kurt Cobain later admitted that the situation brought the pair close to suicide. Help, though, in the form of what bassist Chris Novoselic later described as "the touring highlight of the year", was at hand.

The horror stories gave a heavy subtext to the Reading performance – something that was wryly acknowledged when Kurt Cobain put an end to the waiting and was brought onto the stage in a wheelchair, wearing a Courtney-style blonde wig and a three-quarter-length hospital gown. Collapsing out of the chair, he grabbed the mic and said, "You're gonna make it, man. With the support of friends and family, you are gonna make it."

The band, who'd barely played together in two months, were in breathtaking form. From the opening chords of 'Breed' to the breakneck finale 'Territorial Pissings' (suffixed with a snatch of 'The Star-Spangled Banner'), the 25-song set covered all aspects of Nirvana's career. There were obscure single sides, cuts from the pre-fame *Bleach* album, a generous helping of *Nevermind* and an instant new classic in the form of 'All Apologies', which Cobain dedicated to his wife and daughter. He also coerced the crowd into chanting "Courtney, we love you" as a message of solidarity, though the 60,000 drenched but delirious festival-goers needed no encouragement to sing every word of 'Lithium', Nirvana's third and most recent British hit single from *Nevermind*.

"This isn't our last show or anything," Novoselic said at one point during the show. "Yes it is," Cobain responded. And in a way it was, for the Reading show marked the moment when Nirvana's impeccable rock band credentials began to be eclipsed by something infinitely more troublesome, something that, 20 months later, would reach an awful climax with Kurt Cobain's suicide.

"Hearing tens of thousands of people sing along with 'Lithium' was a very cool moment in the history of the band."
CHRIS NOVOSELIC

A New Respectability

NIRVANA AND 'THE SOUND OF SEATTLE' THAT

EXPLODED INTO PUBLIC CONSCIOUSNESS IN THE WAKE OF THE BAND'S SUCCESS, INVIGORATED A GUITAR ROCK SCENE THAT HAD LARGELY FALLEN INTO DISREPAIR, EVEN PARODY. BUT AFTER KURT COBAIN'S SHOCKING DEATH, THE RUSH OF IMITATORS SOON CEASED, LEAVING A MORE DIVERSE — IF NO LESS CONFUSED — MUSICAL CULTURE.

JUST AS THE DEATHS OF BRIAN JONES AND JIMI HENDRIX, JANIS JOPLIN AND JIM MORRISON AT THE TURN OF THE '60S HAD PROMPTED A MASS FLIGHT INTO FANCIFUL GLAM ROCK AND PROGRESSIVE VIRTUOSITY, THE CHUMMY TUNES OF MID-'90S BRITPOP EMERGED TO OBLITERATE COBAIN'S PAINFUL REMINDER OF ROCK'N'ROLL'S CLOSE RELATIONSHIP WITH OBLIVION. AT ONE EXTREME, OASIS AND BLUR EMERGED TRIUMPHANT ON A TIDE OF PECULIARLY BRITSH LADDISHNESS, THE EPITOME OF INDIE'S DECADE-LONG PILLAGING OF PAST MUSICAL STYLES. OASIS IN PARTICULAR WENT FOR THE JUGULAR, INSERTING ELEMENTS FREELY DRAWN FROM T. REX AND THE SEX PISTOLS INTO THEIR MID-'60S BEATLES CORE. PULP TOOK THE PLAUDITS FOR QUIRKY ORIGINALITY, THOUGH, THEIR 'COMMON PEOPLE' SINGLE, RAPTUROUSLY RECEIVED AT THEIR 1995 GLASTONBURY APPEARANCE, BECOMING THE ERA'S KEY ANTHEM.

WHILE ARTISTS SUCH AS BJÖRK AND EMINEM CONFIRM THAT CONTEMPORARY MUSIC REMAINS A BROAD CHURCH, PERHAPS THE MOST SURPRISING ELEMENT IN RECENT YEARS HAS BEEN THE REHABILITATION OF ROCK'S SENIOR CITIZENS, WHICH ECHOES THE REVERENCE ASPIRING R&B GROUPS IN THE '60S HAD FOR THE OLD BLUES MASTERS. SO IT'S ENTIRELY FITTING THAT THE BOOK CLOSES WITH BRIAN WILSON. THE MAN BEHIND THE BEACH BOYS HITS, WILSON'S MAINSTREAM SUCCESS IS JUST ONE FACET OF A CAREER THAT HAS SEEN HIM RESCUED FROM THE BRINK OF MADNESS, AND HAILED AS POP'S PREMIER COMPOSER THANKS TO HIS *SMILE* PROJECT, BROUGHT BACK TO LIFE AFTER AN EXTRAORDINARY ABSENCE OF 37 YEARS. A SYMBOL BOTH OF POP'S CREATIVE AND DESTRUCTIVE URGES, BRIAN WILSON WAS MOST DEFINITELY THERE. OUT THERE!

256   **Jeff Buckley, Sin-é, New York, 1993**

JEFF BUCKLEY
SIN-É, ST MARK'S PLACE, EAST VILLAGE, NEW YORK, 19 JULY 1993

The estranged son of Tim Buckley, the hippie-era troubadour who died in 1975, Jeff Buckley inherited both his father's vocal elasticity and extraordinary good looks. Releasing his first album *Grace* in 1994, Buckley seemed poised for greatness before the spectre of his father returned on 29 May 1997 when Jeff, too, died tragically young, in a drowning accident in the Mississippi River.

A performer who was able to stun an audience into silence simply by taking a sharp intake of breath, Buckley perfected his trade in a small café/bar in New York's East Village, a regular haunt of his from spring 1992 until the following summer. In the audience on many occasions was friend and photographer Merri Cyr:

"I first saw him there in Fall 1992. Sin-é was a small coffee house owned by these Irish guys. There was no stage, just a spotlight, a mic and a lousy sound system. Initially, there wasn't even any alcohol; they just sold cappuccinos. If you wanted a drink, you went next door.

"You had to be pretty good to make yourself sound good there, but Jeff was amazing. Even at this early stage, he had a really great voice, and he was a great mimic. He could sing a song like Nina Simone's 'Be Your Husband' with all the depth and spirituality of a 50-year-old black woman. Girls blubbed when he sang Leonard Cohen's 'Hallelujah'.

> # He could sing a song like Nina Simone's 'Be Your Husband' with all the depth and spirituality of a 50-year-old black woman.
> ## MERRI CYR, PHOTOGRAPHER

"Not long after I first saw him, Jeff got signed by Columbia. The label hired the place out on 19 July 1993 so they could record him in familiar surroundings. Jeff was very nervous in the afternoon, though for the evening set, he invited all his friends and the pressure was off a bit. He must have played for at least four hours that day.

"Jeff had this big voice but he was most powerful when he sang quietly. Sometimes, he'd start in this real quiet whisper and people would instantly shut up. He was very tuned in to the vibe of an audience. He would do this thing at the beginning of a show, like he was smelling the air to get the mood of the crowd.

"Jeff Buckley found himself musically when he played Sin-é. He regarded the place as a home from home. He'd stop by during the day and have coffee, and develop what he was doing musically by night. They liked him there so he could pretty much play what and when he wanted. You just watched him grow week to week."

Jeff Buckley, Sin-é, New York, 1993

Jeff Buckley found himself a 'home away from home' in Sin-é. The recording of the legendary gig has helped seal Jeff Buckley's cult status and cement his reputation as one of the finest performers of his generation.

Left: Please allow me to introduce myself . . .
Bono as MacPhisto.
Above: MacPhisto meets Rushdie.
Right: MacPhisto toys with bassist Adam
Clayton.

U2
WEMBLEY STADIUM, LONDON, 11 AUGUST 1993

Having thrust themselves onto the international stage with 1987's *The Joshua Tree*, U2's highly textured, gestural rock could easily have fallen out of fashion when Nirvana and the Seattle sound arrived in 1991 to return rock to its baser roots. The band's response was to temper their Eighties-style production bluster, embrace dance beats'n'bleeps and dramatically overhaul their stage show to meet the media-savvy standards of the era. By the time of 1993's *Zooropa*, U2 had transformed themselves from an epic rock band into an all-encompassing media spectacle, where pop and postmodernism collided – and Bono got to call himself MacPhisto.

Ostensibly the European leg of the previous year's *Zoo* tour, the *Zooropa* tour – which was launched in Rotterdam in May 1993 – featured banks of television screens that broadcast nightly news bulletins from war-torn Sarajevo, suggestive slogans and messages, and some mystifying "art" imagery. A theatre troupe appeared on stage dressed as U2 – and then there was ringmaster Bono, a debauched, Presley-like character in devil's horns and a gold lamé

suit, providing a wry commentary on celebrity and seemingly anything else that mattered. Bono's star turn, though, was the moment when he'd interrupt each show and get on the phone. The audience eavesdropped nightly on his one-to-one chats with anyone from American President Bill Clinton to Irish vocal group Clannad.

When the extravaganza hit Wembley (on the first of four nights there), Bono had a real ace up his sleeve. That night's phone pal was Salman Rushdie, author of 1989's *The Satanic Verses*, and the subject of a fatwa (death sentence) prompted by the book's supposedly disrespectful take on Islamic religion. In fact Rushdie, a cause célebre for liberals and intellectuals who'd spent the previous four years in hiding, wasn't just at the end of the phone. He was backstage and, when he walked out front, he was given a hero's welcome. MacPhisto knelt at his feet, kissed Rushdie's hand, the pair embraced and then the rarely sighted author was gone. Point made: the show, the most remarkable stadium extravaganza of its time, must go on.

"Look what you've done to me. You've made me very famous and I thank you. I know you like your pop stars to be exciting so I bought these [points to his golden shoes]. Now my time among you is almost at an end, the glory of ZOOTV must ascend and take its place with all the other satellites. Don't fear, for I'll be watching you..."

BONO AS MACPHISTO

"Noel rounded everyone up, took their backstage passes and said, 'Let's give 'em to the kids."
PAUL SLATTERY,
PHOTOGRAPHER

"I'd been in the business 20 years, but this was one of the best gigs I'd seen in my life. To see a band that hot, in that kind of club, with that kind of atmosphere was amazing.

"It was Oasis's 63rd gig since February that year, during which time they'd gone from playing pubs to Glastonbury in June, then on to bigger venues such as The Forum in London. They were really looking forward to Japan. They'd got wind from Sony that it was gonna be massive, it was their first long haul trip, and it totally removed them from all the controversy at home, all that hype surrounding the [*Definitely Maybe*] album. For those six or seven days, it was like being on another planet.

"They'd been booked into these small Club Quattros, a chain of venues that hold 600–700 people, though they could have sold out each gig several times over. They started off with three nights in Tokyo,

played one in Osaka, and then ended up in Nagoya. By the time of the final show, fans were following them round on trains, booking into the same hotels, and showering them with all kinds of presents. People had come from all over Japan to buy tickets for that last night. So Noel rounded everyone up, took their backstage passes and said, 'Let's give 'em to the kids.' Oasis are cynical at the best of times, but Japan totally chilled them out. There was this kind of mutual love going on...

"Right from the start of the show, you could sense the excitement. I remember Liam walking on, looking out and saying, 'Fuckin' hell!' Then the band launched into the set – 'Rock'n'Roll Star' followed by 'Columbia' and 'Fade Away' – and it was mindblowing. I was crammed in this tiny little pit, between the band and the crowd, trying to take photographs amidst all this

pandemonium. It was totally packed, totally sweaty, but nobody was being aggressive. Japanese fans are enthusiastic without being nuts.

Noel's short acoustic set came as a relief to everyone. We were all desperate for a five-minute break and a beer. I went backstage and there was Guigsy sitting there, drenched, with a towel round his head, just stunned by it all. Later on, during 'I Am The Walrus', I touched my head and I swear my hair was standing on end. The song ended, and everyone started to cry, even the band! Maybe I was crying too. Liam rarely smiled on stage, but this time he was grinning from ear to ear. And I'd never seen Oasis play an encore before, but they came back, did 'Rock'n'Roll Star' again, and the place completely erupted. It was mega, an absolutely brilliant gig."

Paul Slattery, photographer

264   **Oasis, Nagoya, Japan, 1994**

Opposite: Overcome with
emotion, band members
shed real tears at the climax
of the Nagoya show.

Above: The Oasis frontline
in full flow.

Right: Even Bonehead
couldn't believe the scenes.
"There was this mutual love
thing going on," says
photographer Paul Slattery.

Oasis, Nagoya, Japan, 1994   265

PULP
GLASTONBURY FESTIVAL, SOMERSET, 24 JUNE 1995

When The Stones Roses pulled out of the Saturday night headline slot at the last minute, the festival organizers had a hair-tearing few moments before someone had the bright idea of booking Pulp. Then in the ascendant with their latest single, 'Common People', the band – and the song – instantly wrote themselves into modern folklore, as 40,000 drenched but exhilarated souls sang along to Jarvis Cocker's irresistibly witty and rousing commentary on class-obsessed Britain.

The audience sang along to 'Common People', they sang along in the hope they might just pull through.

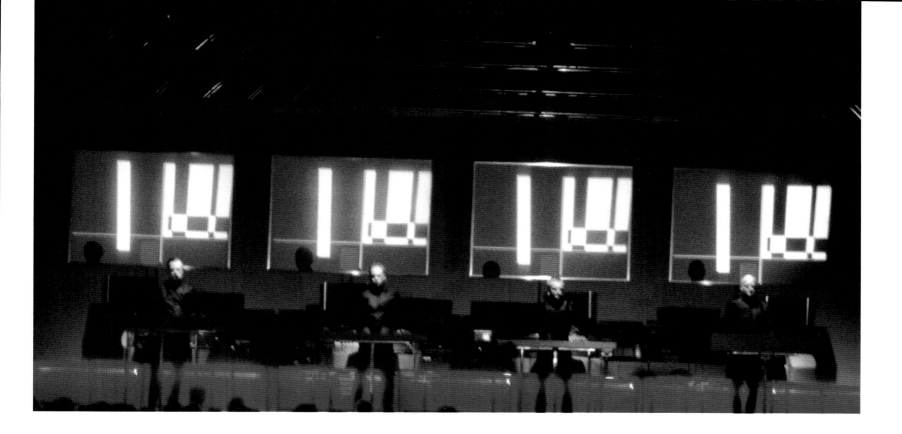

KRAFTWERK
TRIBAL GATHERING, LUTON HOO, 24 MAY 1997

The ultimate acid house party under the stars, Tribal Gathering grew out of the early rave scene, paving the way for a variety of imitators. It reached its apotheosis in 1997 when the organizers tempted Kraftwerk back out of a five-year semi-retirement to play in a giant field in the Home Counties.

Still fronted by cycling enthusiast Ralf Hütter, the one-time architecture student largely responsible for sculpting the group's sound and austere look, Kraftwerk lived up to their billing as, in the words of NME's Simon Witter, "the most influential white group in the history of dance music". Acolytes such as Orbital and Daft Punk might have found themselves higher up the bill, but it was the stoic-looking quartet of man-machines that remained determinedly static against the slogans and images projected behind them who stole the headlines.

"As the set proceeds from one pristine electronic landmark to another – 'Numbers', 'Man Machine', an incandescently lovely 'Tour De France' – there's no resisting the conclusion that the reason Kraftwerk's live set has remained essentially unchanged since 1987 is that you can't improve upon perfection," wrote Ben Thompson in MOJO magazine.

Kraftwerk, Tribal Gathering, Luton Hoo, 1997   267

RADIOHEAD
GLASTONBURY FESTIVAL, 28 JUNE 1997

Expectations for Radiohead's homecoming performance were understandably high. After all, *OK Computer*, the band's just released third album, had been getting extraordinary reviews. However, faced with the prospect of playing five huge outdoor shows in quick succession, singer Thom Yorke was not entirely filled with confidence. "I can't see why we're doing these big gigs," he complained. "It's not something I'm emotionally capable of yet." Drawing both on *OK Computer* and the band's previous album, *The Bends*, the set list was a virtual wet dream, from the opening dreamscape 'Lucky' through the deliciously meandering 'Paranoid Android' to the sublime 'Street Spirit (Fade Out)' encore. They even played their alternative national anthem, 'Creep', despite the fact that they had long grown tired of it. However, it could all have gone horribly wrong.

Little over halfway through the show, as Radiohead were about to launch into 'Talk Show Host', the monitors began to play up. Yorke began missing his cues. The band looked confused. The singer, a beautiful, fragile soul at the best of times, was close to walking off stage, something that seemed a dead cert when the footlights began to shine directly into his eyes. Miraculously, the dread moment passed. The sound cleared up. Yorke bawled at the lighting man to turn the lights towards the crowd. As the audience literally lit up, Radiohead reignited. There was something almost religious about the transition, an epiphany that seemed to affect everyone who witnessed it. Years later, *Q* magazine nominated Radiohead's Glastonbury performance as the best gig ever.

"Everything after [Glastonbury] has been a letdown. I've never felt like that. It wasn't a human feeling." THOM YORKE

Opposite: Frontman Thom Yorke was close to walking
off stage before the band turned their performance round.
Above: Radiohead guitar whizz Jonny Greenwood.

Woodstock 99
Rome, New York State, 23–25 July 1999

"30 Years Of Peace And Music," declared the posters that welcomed the 200,000-plus crowd that made its way towards a decommissioned air force base in upstate New York. However, by the end of the three-day festival, all the talk was not of peace and love, but profit and violence. Woodstock '99 climaxed in a plague of fires with gangs of fans on the rampage and, in the days that followed, several incidents of rape and sexual abuse emerged to drag the event even further into the rock'n'roll doldrums.

It had all started with such promise. Just as in 1969, Woodstock '99 witnessed a gathering of the tribes, various strands of what are popularly called alternative lifestyles. The beads and beards had been replaced by a proliferation of tattoos and body piercing, and while some again chose to go naked, they were more likely to be seen whizzing round bareback on a skateboard than flat on their back in a state of blissful serenity.

When James Brown kicked off the festival on Friday afternoon, the crowd was as one, its hands collectively raised and clapping along with the funk godfather's insistent rhythms. By Saturday night, the mood had changed drastically. It was during sets by Korn and Limp Bizkit on this loudest of days that two of the alleged rapes took place, both in and around the mosh pits – which tended to resemble war zones at the best of times.

It was the events of the following night that stole the early headlines, though, when a group of around 250 people created scenes of havoc, igniting at least half a dozen serious fires, trashing dozens of merchandizing stalls and tents, and pulling down speaker towers.

The festival closed, as arranged, with Jimi Hendrix's chilling version of 'The Star-Spangled Banner' from Woodstock '69 broadcast on giant video screens. The guitarist's violent reworking of the American National anthem, originally aimed at the White House warmongers who masterminded the Vietnam fiasco, now provided a chilling soundtrack to the out-of-control children of the Woodstock generation. "The '69 event is not going to change in people's minds because of what happened here. This event had its own particular problems, but positive experiences as well. People had an amazing time for the most part. Of course, there are things you just can't tolerate, such as the assaults on women," said Michael Lang, co-organizer of Woodstock 1969 and 1999.

Below left: Flea from Red Hot Chili Peppers.
Below right: Rage Against the Machine.
Opposite: The 30th anniversary Woodstock began in a riot of colour and ended in a blaze of chaos and destruction.

Woodstock '99 saw more than 1,200 tons of solid waste and 500,000 gallons of liquid waste tumble down more than 2,500 on-site "portajohns".

Eminem is the all-American anti-hero. "I am whatever you say I am," he says, dipping in and out of characters with all the dash of his rapid-fire rhymes. Bringing a Sid Vicious-style white trash aesthetic to hip-hop, Marshall Mathers from "Hicksville, Bumfuck", otherwise known as Detroit's East Side, once honed his free-styling talents at Maurice Malone's Hip-Hop shop.

By 2000, he was filling out stadiums and utilizing various theatrical devices to enhance his Eminem persona. None was more controversial than the chainsaw, an emblem of murderous violence thanks to horror flick *The Texas Chainsaw Massacre*, that had its Swedish makers up in arms and claiming: "We make chainsaws for mature people who have genuine forestry work to do." Some local authorities invoked health and safety legislation and banned him from switching the machine on. One or two demanded that the machine's "teeth" be removed. All the while, Public Enemy Number One just got more popular still.

"We make chainsaws for mature people who have genuine forestry work to do." HUSQVARN, MAKERS OF CHAINSAWS

MANIC STREET PREACHERS
TEATRO KARL MARX, HAVANA, CUBA, 17 FEBRUARY 2001

**Opposite: Manics' guitarist and singer
James Dean Bradfield.
Below: Bradfield (left), bassist Nicky Wire
and drummer Sean Moore meet
Fidel Castro and his interpreter.**

They've hardly been starved of music in Cuba, but rock'n'roll, once denounced by the Communist republic authorities as a "decadent influence", has been slow to find its way into the nation's culture. Only in December 2000, when Fidel Castro unveiled a statue to the late John Lennon and acknowledged him as "a revolutionary", did things begin to change.

Almost instantly, the Manic Street Preachers cooked up a visit to the Caribbean's lone bulwark against the irrepressible march of capitalism. With their politically charged songs, military-style fatigues and anti-American sentiments, it seemed like a perfect fit, though some regarded the venture as merely part of the propaganda war to announce the imminent arrival of their latest album *Know Your Enemy*.

No matter, the Manics were by far the biggest and best band yet to rock Havana (Billy Joel had preceded them). Prior to the show, they had an audience with the Cuban leader, before performing to a packed house of 5,000 – each of whom had paid the equivalent of 17 pence for a ticket.

"Cuba is the last symbol that really fights against the Americanization of the world," said bassist Nicky Wire in a snub to the critics. The Manics said it with music, too: one of their latest songs, 'Baby Elian', had been inspired by the kidnapping of a young, motherless Cuban boy by his Miami-based relatives, a dispute that ended with the boy being returned to his father in Cuba.

"Noel Gallagher goes to meet Tony f**king Blair and we meet Fidel Castro." NICKY WIRE

Manic Street Preachers, Havana, Cuba, 2001

> ## "The White Stripes were breaking everything down to its bare bones."
> ### STEVIE CHICK

THE WHITE STRIPES
FAT TUESDAY'S, AUSTIN, TEXAS, 17 MARCH 2001

"The *NME* sent me to South By Southwest (SXSW) in Austin, Texas, to write a feature on Elbow. I knew that each year squads of weird bands descend on the place, and that once I'd done the interview, I wanted to catch as many of them as I could.

"One afternoon, as I was waiting outside a tattoo parlour while some friends were getting tattooed, I heard this slide guitar coming from across the road. I thought, that sounds a lot like The White Stripes. I called out to [*NME* photographer] Steve Gullick and said, 'Let's see this band, it sounds fantastic.' A few months earlier, a friend of mine who knew I liked garage rock had sent me a copy of their second album *De Stijl* with a post-it note that said, 'Guess what? Next year, two-piece blues bands will be the biggest thing in rock'n'roll.' He was joking, really, but I was blown away, both by the energy and Jack White's songwriting.

"The venue was an open-air area at the back of a bar. The occasion was a launch party for what became a failed dot com venture. And there must have been three, maybe four hundred people there. The White Stripes weren't even headlining. Preston School Of Industry, a Pavement side project, topped the bill. But it was the most important show I ever attended, not least because I became the first person to review them in the UK.

"I went over the top, but I still stick by what I wrote. It felt as if rock'n'roll was being reborn, that The White Stripes were breaking everything down to its bare bones. Indie rock was sounding so false. Nothing was blowing me away as much as MC5 and The Stooges. I felt that The White Stripes had gone back and taken all this surface nonsense away. The references weren't tiny indie bands. They were an extraordinary two-piece who spliced the blues and heavy rock, and had a clumpy bass drum that made it sound a bit like hip-hop.

"The third song they played was a cover of Dolly Parton's 'Jolene', and it was astonishing how Jack got to the heart of the song by scraping away years of kitsch and over-familiarity. Steve looked at me and said, 'This is amazing!' Then he leapt up on stage and started taking pictures.

"We came back raving about them, but the mag still hadn't run my review of the album. I guess they didn't think there was much of a future for a two-piece blues band from Detroit. We managed to browbeat the new live editor into letting us run a review of the gig, together with a picture, though no one could have predicted how huge it would be just months later."

Stevie Chick, journalist

BJÖRK

Few "pop" artists could gatecrash the home of the English National Opera and transform its rarefied setting into a perfectly natural habitat. But in a unique feat of sound and theatre, that's exactly what Björk did, a climax of sorts to a 15-year career that had seen her develop from a punk-inspired singer with The Sugarcubes into a composer/performer of extraordinary passion and innate peculiarity. The highlight of a world tour of "serious" music venues to promote her latest album, *Vespertine*, the Coliseum show also struck a blow to the old high art/popular culture divide.

Despite the fact that tickets – at between £30 and £50 – were fixed at distinctly "high culture" prices, the genuine eclecticism of Björk's performance was drawn from all parts of the cultural spectrum. "To make something magical is easy," she said at the time, and that's exactly how it looked. A more traditionally minded artist might have baulked at the prospect of bringing together a 15-strong Inuit choir, hi-tech synth rhythms from electronica duo Matmos, a harp player and a north Canadian throat singer named

"To make something magical is easy." BJÖRK

Tagag, not to mention the tiny Icelandic singer herself, with a voice every bit as elastic as the sounds behind her. However, such a richly layered ensemble seemed entirely in keeping with Björk's idiosyncratic vision.

Visually, too, the show was stunning. Against a huge video backdrop of Arctic landscapes and biological images, the nymph-like singer in her feather-festooned Alexander McQueen dress utilized her body to match the music's playful extravagance. Better still was the absence of a conventional rock group. Instead, the opening spectacle of Björk, spotlit in a chair, turning the tiny handle of an antique musical box while feathers fell like snow around her, belied the musical paradises that were about to unfold.

After a first half largely made up of songs from the new album, Björk returned after the interval with a more crowd-pleasing set that included 'Bachelorette' (where she forgot her lines), the woefully underrated 'Hyperballad', and encores of 'Army Of Me' and 'Human Behaviour'. The show ended in typically unfamiliar fashion, though, with the audience clapping along with the Inuit choir on a song most had never even heard before.

Just yards away were the tombs of Lenin and Stalin.

It was, joked The *Moscow Times*, the beginning of a new partnership: Lenin and McCartney. However, those two old revolutionaries, Lenin and Lennon, were long gone, as was the USSR, which Paul McCartney had sung about with such passion back in the Cold War days – but not The Beatles, apparently, whose music provided the bulk of McCartney's first ever concert in Russia.

"I've long wanted to play in Russia, but for a number of years, when the Communists were in power, they didn't want me to," said McCartney when the date was announced. "I've never even visited Russia as a tourist, so it's exciting for me now to be getting to perform there with a band and finally be singing 'Back In The USSR' and all these other songs for people, who, I've got a feeling, might be ready for it," he added.

Though not banned outright in the old USSR, Beatles records were certainly difficult to come by. Then when relations with the West first began to thaw, McCartney released *CHOBA B CCCP* (alias *Back In The USSR*), a 1988 Soviet Union-only collection of old rock'n'roll cover versions.

McCartney's longstanding interest in the country and its people was rewarded when a crowd of around 20,000 descended on Moscow's famous Red Square to catch the ex-Beatle towards the end of his lengthy world tour. Shouts of "We love you, Paul!" filled

PAUL McCARTNEY
RED SQUARE, MOSCOW, 24 MAY 2003

the air, just yards away from the tombs of the founding fathers of the Soviet Union, Lenin and Stalin. (Inevitably, there had been objections to the concert taking place on such hallowed old Soviet ground.)

Before the show, McCartney had enjoyed a private audience in the Kremlin with President Putin, who told him that The Beatles had been "like a breath of fresh air, like a window on the outside world". McCartney responded with an impromptu version of 'Let It Be' – Putin was unable to attend the evening concert – and said it was "nice to see the reality" of what had been to him "a mystical land. I always suspected that people had big hearts. Now I know that's true."

In front of banks of video screens displaying footage from his Beatles glory days, McCartney kicked off his show with 'Hello Goodbye', ending it over 30 songs later with a medley of 'Sgt Pepper's Lonely Hearts Club Band' and 'The End'. And, yes, he played 'Back In The USSR' – twice.

BRIAN WILSON

A staggering 36 years after it had been written off as an unworkable vanity project by a crackpot prodigy, *Smile*, Brian Wilson's great unfinished mid-20th-century symphony, was unveiled in a series of instantly legendary shows in London. A virtual note-for-note facsimile based on original recordings made in 1966 and 1967, this extraordinary project dragged pop kicking and screaming into timeless territory.

Happily – for the man endured his share of troubles down the years – Wilson was still around to perform his recovered opus together with a vast band, including horn and string sections, put together by musical director and co-founder of The Wondermints Darian Sahanaja.

Though *Smile* inevitably provided the centrepiece of the show, the night began with a handful of Wilson's hits written for The Beach Boys – poignant, pre-*Smile* classics such as 'Surfer Girl', 'In My Room', 'Please Let Me Wonder' and 'All Summer Long' – done a capella style. In a shift of dynamics, the band then joined him for full-bodied versions of 'Darlin'', 'God Only Knows', 'Sloop John B' and 'California Girls'.

Smile itself sounded no less awe-inspiring than it would have done had it been released, as planned, back in 1967. Its opening 'Americana' suite of songs, from the suitably sacred a capella 'Our Prayer' through to the remarkable 'Cabin Essence', was simply breathtaking. Wilson once claimed he wrote "white spirituals", an assessment that was impossible to dispute as the set continued with the superlatively voiced 'Heroes And Villains', complete with horses' hooves, steam trains and those slide whistles favoured by silent-era funnymen.

A masterful achievement of wordplay and allegory, thanks to lyricist Van Dyke Parks (also present), *Smile* simply got better. Its second suite, a four-part hymn to innocence built around a child-is-father-of-the-man theme, concluded with 'Surf's Up'. 'Good Vibrations', quite possibly three-minute pop's most extraordinary achievement, brought the final section of *Smile* to a close. There were few dry eyes left in the house. A closing medley of 'Barbara Ann' and 'Surfin'' USA' was a reminder that Brian Wilson was also the master of uncomplicated, fun-based pop, as well as sublime tapestries of sonic delights.

"*Smile* is the most important piece of music that I ever composed. I hope that the music makes everybody smile." BRIAN WILSON

INDEX

ACKNOWLEDGEMENTS

Many thanks to the following, real live interviewees:
Daevid Allen, Roberta Bayley, Stevie Chick, Petula Clark, John Coleman, Merri Cyr, Jeff Dexter, Vic Godard, John 'Hoppy' Hopkins, Jane Wilson, Joan Jara, Peter Jenner, Simon Klein, Erika Lewis, Nick Mason, Mike McInnerney, Martin O'Neill, Ron Pownall, Mick Rock, Captain Sensible, Rob Simmons, Siouxsie Sioux, Paul Slattery, John Stanley, Simone Stenfors, Donna Suffling, Rick Wakeman, Roger Waters, Mick 'Woody' Woodmansey, Mary Woronov.

And a big hand to:
Pat Andrews, Martin Barden, Simon Benham, Joe Black at Universal Music, Geoff Brown, Rob Byron at Steel Wheels, Rick Conrad at Warner Bros, Andy Davis, Fred Dellar, Peter Doggett, Daryl Easlea, Lora Findlay, Julie-Anne Fraser, Pat Gilbert, Johnny Greene (at GAS), John Harding, Phil King, Trevor King, Erika Lewis, Martha and Tara, Maddy Miller, Pauline Murray, Andy Neill, Bernice Owen, Norman Paytress, Donatella Piccinetti, Rei, John Reed, Simon Robinson, Harvir Sahota, Neil Scaplehorn at Ace Records, Eugenia Borajo Serra, Kate Simon, Cristina Szabo, Kieron Tyler, Monica Cano Villaverde, Louise Voss, Alan Williams, Lois Wilson.

Thanks to Zoë Holtermann for her intrepid picture research, and to Anna Cheifetz and everyone else at Cassell Illustrated. And first and foremost, to Joanne Wilson, my editor at Cassell Illustrated, for commissioning the book and seeing it through with all the necessary patience and good humour. Extra special thanks to Dave Brolan for additional picture research.

Mark Paytress, May 2005

Sources:
P 52 Rolling Stones pull-quote: Norman Jopling (*Record Mirror*).
P 101 Jim Morrison pull-quote: John Tobler (*Zigzag*).
P 103 Wayne Kramer quoted text: (*MOJO*, 2003).
P 224 Freddie Mercury pull-quote: (*Record Mirror*, 1985).
P 194 George Clinton pull-quote: Toby Manning (*Q*, 2004).
P 246 Kurt Cobain pull-quote: Everett True (*Melody Maker*, 1992).

The publishers are grateful to the following:
Mark Veznaver for the idea, Dave Brolan for help with the pictures and Simon at Design 23. Thanks also to Terri Hinte, Daryl Easlea, Zoë at Mute records, Mark Fenwick, Sue Bosanko, Michelle Pickering, Ruth Baldwin, Liz Fowler and Sophie Delpech.

Thanks to everyone who provided pictures especially all the individual contributors and photographers mentioned below. Special thanks to Zoë Holtermann.